OpenCart 4: Dev Guide for Themes & Extensions

Unlock the Potential of OpenCart 4: Master Theme, Extension Development, and Docs for the Developers

RUPAK NEPALI

ISBN: 9798324513375

DEDICATION AND ACKNOWLEDGMENTS

I would like to extend my deepest gratitude to everyone who has supported and inspired me throughout the journey of creating this book, OpenCart 4: Dev Guide for Themes & Extensions.

To the OpenCart community, thank you for your constant innovation, collaboration, and dedication. Your contributions and insights have significantly shaped the content of this book. I am grateful to the developers, testers, and users who have continually pushed the boundaries of what is possible with OpenCart.

Firstly, my heartfelt thanks go to my wife, Le Ann Lennan. Your unwavering support, patience, and encouragement have been the cornerstone of this endeavor. Your belief in me and your understanding during the late nights and long weekends have been truly invaluable. I would also like to acknowledge my family and friends for their continuous support and encouragement. Your positivity and belief in my work have motivated me to strive for excellence.

Lastly, a big thank you to all the readers and fellow developers. Your passion for learning and improving e-commerce solutions inspires me every day. I hope this book serves as a valuable resource in your journey with OpenCart.

To the vibrant OpenCart community—thank you for your contributions, insights, and camaraderie. Together, we build a brighter future for online commerce.

Join us at https://webocreation.com to download the complete code example and you can also ask questions and comment about this book or other Opencart and eCommerce blog posts. You can submit or report issues, and errata and seek additional advice. You can also directly email us at webocreation.com@gmail.com

Rupak Nepali
https://webocreation.com

Some assumptions:
The **oc_** prefix is used in all database table names, in your case it may be different which you can find in config.php.
Codes are in italics.
All images have a caption that starts with **Fig:** and we reference them on multiple pages as needed
Used https://demo.webocreation.com as the main Opencart store
All codes are available at GitHub repo Opencart-free-modules https://github.com/rupaknepali/Opencart-free-modules

TABLE OF CONTENTS

Choose a better hosting provider and better cache module

Defer all the extra CSS and JS at the footer.

Use the image sizes properly

Use the proper extension for the image:

Optimize the image properly

Lazy loading of images:

GZIP compression level

Speed up the repeat visit by serving static assets with an efficient cache policy

Compress and minify the o1-year

Minify your HTML, CSS, and JS

Index the database table

Developer or Designer tasks: Ensure text remains visible during Webfont load

Caching

CDN - setup Cloudflare easily for eCommerce websites

15. OPENCART SECURITY MEASURES

Use good and secure hosting

Check if the install/ folder is still there

Proper Security settings in the admin

Use HTTPS/SSL Certificate

Use the latest PHP version

Use Anti-fraud extension

Error handling setting

Monitor your admin error logs

Block bad bots

Allowed File extensions and allowed file mime type permissions

Review All Users, User Groups, and Grant the Minimum Permissions Necessary

Use a strong username and password

API security in Opencart

Always use the latest Opencart version, theme, modules, and extensions

Remove unused modules or extensions

Monitor your server logs

Use HTTP security headers

Cross-Site Scripting (XSS)

Database Security and SQL Injections

Denial of Service

Backup

Use Google Captcha or Basic Captcha

16. OPENCAT VQMOD TUTORIALS

Download:

Installation steps of VqMod for Opencart 4

Configuration:

Errors and Solutions:

Example use of Vqmod in Opencart 4

17. PRO TIPS FOR OPENCART DEVELOPERS

Activating twig debugging

18. COMMON ERRORS AND THEIR SOLUTIONS

Useful Links

1. INTRODUCTION, INSTALLATION, AND FUNDAMENTALS

Opencart is a powerful, user-friendly open-source e-commerce framework that allows businesses to create and manage their online stores with ease. It provides a comprehensive suite of features designed to streamline the process of selling products and services online. OpenCart's flexibility, coupled with its robust set of tools, makes it an excellent choice for small and large businesses. OpenCart 4 introduces several enhancements and new features to improve usability, performance, and security. The OpenCart ecosystem includes a vibrant community of developers, designers, and store owners contributing to the platform's continuous improvement. Additionally, the OpenCart marketplace provides a plethora of themes, extensions, and modules to enhance your online store's functionality and aesthetics.

Key Features of OpenCart

- **Multi-Store Capability**: Manage multiple stores from a single admin interface.
- **Extensive Extensions Library**: Enhance your store's functionality with thousands of available extensions.
- **SEO-Friendly**: Optimize your store for search engines with built-in SEO tools.
- **User Management**: Control access to various store parts with user permissions.
- **Customizable Themes**: Personalize your store's appearance with customizable themes.
- **Multi-Language and Multi-Currency Support**: Cater to a global audience by offering multiple languages and currencies.
- **Comprehensive Reporting**: Gain insights into your store's performance with detailed reports and analytics.
- Besides basic features, multi-language, multi-store, multi-layout, fully customizable, and many more with OCMOD or VqMod virtual file modification with XML and also includes an unlimited module instance system and uses popular foundations like bootstrap, font awesome, and flex slider for rapid development.

Who can use OpenCart?
OpenCart is suitable for many users, including:

- **Small to Medium-Sized Businesses**: Ideal for businesses looking for a cost-effective yet powerful e-commerce solution.

- **Developers and Designers**: Offers a flexible platform that can be extensively customized to meet client needs.
- **E-Commerce Entrepreneurs**: Perfect for individuals launching a new online store due to its user-friendly setup and management.

From the user's perspective

- Creating eCommerce websites
- Launch store simply and faster
- Save investment cost
- Opencart is lightweight
- Handle easier: ideal for end-users to control their Opencart stores
- Catch up with eCommerce trends.

As per the Programmer's Perspective:

- Creating Advanced eCommerce websites
- Easy learning curve, Large Community, and Support
- MVCL (Model View Controller Language)
- Customize the presentation layer or front end
- Flexibility, Customization, and Extend the functionality
- Open Source, Cost-Effective, and many more.

Install Opencart locally, Clone, and Set up Opencart from Github with Docker

To set up a local PHP development environment with Docker for Opencart involves creating a Docker Compose configuration file to define the services needed for running Opencart, such as PHP, MySQL, Redis, Apache, etc. Below is a step-by-step guide to help you set up your development environment:

Install Docker and Docker Compose

Make sure you have Docker and Docker Compose installed on your system. You can download and install them from the official Docker website: https://www.docker.com/get-started

Clone the Opencart Github

Install Git: Before you can clone the Opencart repository, you need to have Git installed on your system. Git is a version control system that allows you to track changes to files and collaborate with others on software development projects. You can download and install Git from the official website: https://git-scm.com/.
Clone the Opencart Repository Once Git is installed, open a terminal or command prompt and navigate to the directory where you want to clone the Opencart repository. Then, run the following command:

git clone https://github.com/Opencart/Opencart.git

This command will clone the entire Opencart repository from GitHub to your local machine.

Set Up a Local Development Environment

To set up a local development environment for Opencart, you'll need a web server (e.g., Apache or Nginx), PHP, and MySQL. You can install these components manually or use a pre-configured solution like Docker.

If you're using Docker, you can create a docker-compose.yml. This file defines the services needed for running Opencart, including PHP, MySQL, and Apache. When you clone from the Opencart Github, everything is already set up for you. You will see docker-compose.yml, Dockerfile, and tools folder

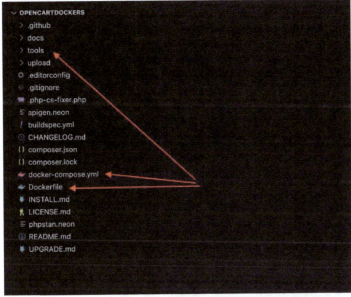

Fig: 1.1

Now, run docker-compose up is the command to start the Docker containers defined in your docker-compose.yml file. This command starts with the services specified in the file, typically including web servers, databases, and any other necessary components for your application.

docker-compose up

The first time will take some time to pull all the Docker images like Postgres, Redis, Memcached, MySQL, Opencart, admirer, etc.

```
[+] Building 1.4s (7/7) FINISHED
 => [opencart internal] load build definition from Dockerfile
 => => transferring dockerfile: 627B
 => [opencart internal] load metadata for docker.io/library/php:8.2-apache
 => [opencart internal] load .dockerignore
 => => transferring context: 2B
 => [opencart 1/3] FROM docker.io/library/php:8.2-apache@sha256:3a2cdc2bd1b62f572d5f8abfc8c069d5bceba0871fb088ebc3f1313ae35dbf75
 => CACHED [opencart 2/3] RUN apt-get update   && apt-get install -y                          wait-for-it                   unzip
 => CACHED [opencart 3/3] RUN a2enmod rewrite
 => [opencart] exporting to image
 => => exporting layers
 => => writing image sha256:3acd05d2b109c17a21e06d7568f2ad9df78a99a8cf3de6aa6fd5f68652e7fe9b
 => => naming to docker.io/library/opencartdocker-opencart
[+] Running 7/7
 ✓ Network opencartdocker_default       Created
 ✓ Container opencartdocker-postgres-1   Created
 ✓ Container opencartdocker-redis-1      Created
 ✓ Container opencartdocker-memcached-1  Created
 ✓ Container opencartdocker-mysql-1      Created
 ✓ Container opencartdocker-opencart-1   Created
 ✓ Container opencartdocker-adminer-1    Created
Attaching to adminer-1, memcached-1, mysql-1, opencart-1, postgres-1, redis-1
```

Fig: 1.2

Once all docker images are pulled, in the end, you will see the Store link and Admin link below:

Fig: 1.3

You can visit http://localhost and you will see the Opencart Store. For admin login go to http://localhost/admin and use admin as username and admin as password.

If you check the Docker Desktop, then you will see the following container:

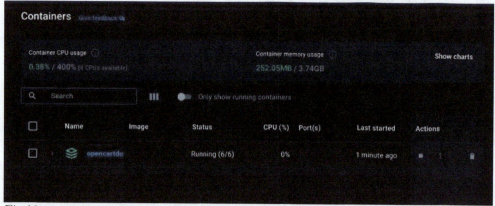

Fig: 14

You will see the following Docker Images pulled:

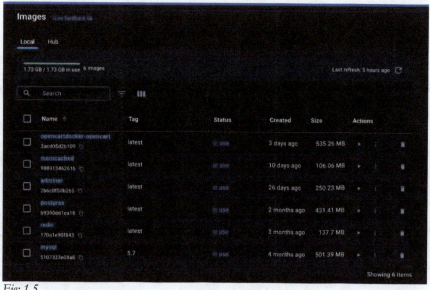

Fig: 1.5

Now you can work in the upload folder code and see changes as you develop in the localhost URL.

Access the Opencart database in Docker

To access the Opencart database visit http://localhost:8080 and enter root as username and password as Opencart.

Fig: 1.6

Once you log in you will see the interface similar to PHPmyadmin, select the Opencart database and you can see all the database tables

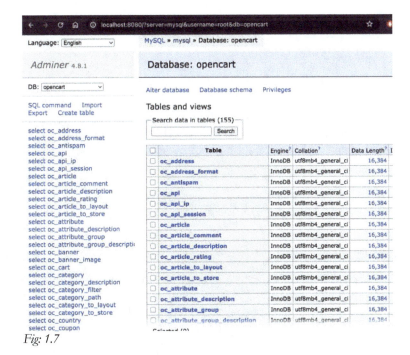

Fig: 1.7

That's it! You now have a local PHP development environment with Docker for Opencart. You can develop and test your Opencart extensions or customizations locally before deploying them to a production environment. If you need it, here are the docker file and the docker-compose file content.

Dockerfile for Opencart

FROM php:8.2.11-apache
ARG DOWNLOAD_URL

```
ARG FOLDER
ENV DIR_OPENCART='/var/www/html/'
ENV DIR_STORAGE='/storage/'
ENV DIR_CACHE=${DIR_STORAGE}'cache/'
ENV DIR_DOWNLOAD=${DIR_STORAGE}'download/'
ENV DIR_LOGS=${DIR_STORAGE}'logs/'
ENV DIR_SESSION=${DIR_STORAGE}'session/'
ENV DIR_UPLOAD=${DIR_STORAGE}'upload/'
ENV DIR_IMAGE=${DIR_OPENCART}'image/'
RUN apt-get clean && apt-get update && apt-get install unzip
RUN apt-get install -y \
  libfreetype6-dev \
  libjpeg62-turbo-dev \
  libpng-dev \
  libzip-dev \
  && docker-php-ext-configure gd --with-freetype --with-jpeg\
  && docker-php-ext-install -j$(nproc) gd \
  && docker-php-ext-install zip && && docker-php-ext-enable zip\
  && docker-php-ext-enable mysqli
RUN apt-get install -y vim
RUN mkdir /storage && mkdir /opencart
RUN if [ -z "$DOWNLOAD_URL" ]; then \
  curl -Lo /tmp/opencart.zip $(sh -c 'curl -s https://api.github.com/repos/opencart/opencart/releases/latest | grep
"browser_download_url" | cut -d : -f 2,3 | tr -d \'"'); \
  else \
  curl -Lo /tmp/opencart.zip ${DOWNLOAD_URL}; \
  fi
RUN unzip /tmp/opencart.zip -d /tmp/opencart;
RUN mv /tmp/opencart/$(if [ -n "$FOLDER" ]; then echo $FOLDER; else unzip -l /tmp/opencart.zip | awk '{print $4}' | grep -
E 'opencart-[a-z0-9.]+/upload/$'; fi)* ${DIR_OPENCART};
RUN rm -rf /tmp/opencart.zip && rm -rf /tmp/opencart && rm -rf ${DIR_OPENCART}install;
RUN mv ${DIR_OPENCART}system/storage/* /storage
COPY configs ${DIR_OPENCART}
COPY php.ini ${PHP_INI_DIR}
RUN a2enmod rewrite
RUN chown -R www-data:www-data ${DIR_STORAGE}
RUN chmod -R 555 ${DIR_OPENCART}
RUN chmod -R 666 ${DIR_STORAGE}
RUN chmod 555 ${DIR_STORAGE}
RUN chmod -R 555 ${DIR_STORAGE}vendor
RUN chmod 755 ${DIR_LOGS}
RUN chmod -R 644 ${DIR_LOGS}*
RUN chown -R www-data:www-data ${DIR_IMAGE}
RUN chmod -R 744 ${DIR_IMAGE}
RUN chmod -R 755 ${DIR_CACHE}
RUN chmod -R 666 ${DIR_DOWNLOAD}
RUN chmod -R 666 ${DIR_SESSION}
RUN chmod -R 666 ${DIR_UPLOAD}
CMD ["apache2-foreground"]
```

Docker Compose Configuration File for Opencart

```
version: '3'
services:
  opencart:
    build: tools
    user: 1000:1000
    ports:
      - "80:80"
    volumes:
      - ./upload:/var/www/html
    depends_on:
      - mysql
    command: >
      bash -c "if [ ! -f /var/www/html/install.lock ]; then
          wait-for-it mysql:3306 -t 60 &&
          cp config-dist.php config.php
          cp admin/config-dist.php admin/config.php
          php /var/www/html/install/cli_install.php install --username admin --password admin --email email@example.com --http_server http://localhost/ --db_driver mysqli --db_hostname mysql --db_username root --db_password opencart --db_database opencart --db_port 3306 --db_prefix oc_;
          touch /var/www/html/install.lock;
      fi &&
          apache2-foreground"
  mysql:
    image: mysql:5.7
    ports:
      - "3306:3306"
    environment:
      - MYSQL_ROOT_PASSWORD=opencart
      - MYSQL_DATABASE=opencart
  adminer:
    image: adminer:latest
    environment:
      ADMINER_DEFAULT_SERVER: mysql
    depends_on:
      - mysql
    ports:
      - "8080:8080"
  redis:
    image: redis:latest
  memcached:
    image: memcached:latest
  postgres:
    image: postgres:latest
    environment:
      - POSTGRES_USER=postgres
      - POSTGRES_PASSWORD=opencart
      - POSTGRES_DB=opencart
```

Coding Standards

Opencart has its coding standards which are designed to ensure consistency and readability across the platform. Adhering to these standards is crucial for maintaining compatibility and ease of collaboration with other developers.

Use MVCL Architecture

Opencart follows the Model-View-Controller (MVC) architecture, which separates the application logic into three interconnected components:

Controller: Acts as an intermediary between models and views. Use controllers to handle user inputs and requests, update models, and load views.

Model: Handles data and business logic. Use models to interact with the database and perform CRUD operations.

View: Manages the presentation layer. Use views to render HTML and present data to the user.

Language: Manages all the language variables

By adhering to the MVCL architecture, you can ensure a clean separation of concerns, making your code more modular and easier to maintain.

Leverage Opencart Events

Opencart has an events system that allows you to hook into various points of the application lifecycle. Using events, you can extend or modify core functionality without altering the core files, ensuring your customizations are upgrade-safe.

Adding Events: Use the addEvent method to register your event listeners in your extension's controller.

Handling Events: Create event listeners that respond to specific events and perform the desired actions.

In Chapter 5, we detail all about Opencart events.

Write Secure Code: Security is paramount in e-commerce development. Ensure your code is secure by following these practices:

Validate User Input: Always validate and sanitize user input to prevent SQL injection, XSS, and other common attacks.

Use Prepared Statements: When interacting with the database, use prepared statements to protect against SQL injection.

Escape Output: Escape all output to prevent cross-site scripting (XSS) attacks.

Optimize Performance

Performance is critical for a smooth user experience. Follow these tips to optimize your Opencart store:

Caching: Implement caching for frequently accessed data to reduce database load and improve response times. Here is one simple example of how a product query is cached with $this->cache->set and get with $this->cache->get

```
$key = md5($sql);
$product_data = $this->cache->get('product.' . $key);
if (!$product_data) {
        $query = $this->db->query($sql);
        $product_data = $query->rows;
        $this->cache->set('product.' . $key, $product_data);
}
```

Minimize HTTP Requests: Combine and minify CSS and JavaScript files to reduce the number of HTTP requests.

Optimize Images: Compress and resize images to reduce load times.

Document Your Code

Clear documentation is essential for maintaining and scaling your projects. Document your code with comments and create comprehensive documentation for your extensions and customizations.

Inline Comments: Use inline comments to explain complex logic and code sections.

Function and Class Comments: Provide detailed descriptions of the purpose and usage of functions and classes.

Stay Updated with Opencart code changes

Opencart is continuously evolving, with new features and security patches being released regularly. Stay updated with the latest versions of Opencart and extensions to ensure compatibility and security.

Naming Convention

All PHP files except view/template files have the extension .php and all view/template files have the extension .twig Line feeds are handled automatically by Git, and the repo is managed using LF. When cloning all line feeds will be converted automatically to your native environment (CRLF for Windows, LF for Mac/Linux).

PHP Tags

Short PHP opening tags and ASP tags are not supported. The characters should be lowercase.

```
<?php
```

All PHP files must include a closing tag for versions before 2.0. PHP files in and after 2.0 will no longer have a closing tag.

```
?>
```

Indentation

PHP files must be indented using the TAB character. 4 space tabs are not supported. HTML in template files (.twig) must be indented using 2 spaces, not 4 spaces or TABS. JavaScript must be indented using the TAB character.

Spacing

IF, WHILE, FOR, etc should have a space before and after the brackets.

Correct **if () {**

Incorrect **if(){**

ELSE etc should have a space after and before the curly braces

Correct **} else {**

Incorrect **}else{**

Type casting does NOT have a space before the variable

Correct **(int)$var**

Incorrect **(int) $var**

Setting a variable should always have a space before and after the equals sign

Correct **$var = 1;**

Incorrect **$var=1;**

Whitespace

After any code, but before a new line - there should be no white space. The same is true for an empty line. After the closing PHP tag, it is essential to remove any white space.

New Lines

Opening curly braces do not go onto a new line, they will always have a space before and be on the same line.

Correct **if ($my_example == 1) {**

Correct **class Product extends \Opencart\System\Engine\Model {**

Correct **public function addExample() {**

Correct **} else {**

Incorrect

if ($my_example == 1)

{

```
class ModelExampleExample extends Model

{

public function addExample()

{

}

else

{
```

File naming

All files should be in lowercase and words separated by an underscore.

Namespaces & Class & Method Naming

Namespaces

Correct: namespace Opencart\Admin\Controller\Common;
Correct: namespace Opencart\Catalog\Controller\Common;

Class names and method names should be camelcase.

Correct **class Controllername extends \Opencart\System\Engine\Controller**

Correct **public function addExample()**

Incorrect **class model_exampleexample extends Model** Correct: **public function add_example()**

A method scope should always be cast.

Correct **public function addExample()** Incorrect **function addExample()**

PHP Function (helpers) naming

Helper function names should be lowercase and an underscore should be used to separate words.

PHP variable naming

PHP variables should be lowercase and an underscore should be used to separate words.

Correct **$var = 123;** Correct **$new_var = 12345;**

Incorrect **$Var = 123;** Incorrect **$newVar = 12345;**

User-defined constants

User-defined constants are set as upper case.

Correct **define('MY_VAR', 'My constant string value');**

Incorrect **define('my_var', 'My constant string value');**

PHP constants

These types of constants (true, false, null) are set as lowercase

Correct **$my_var = true;** Incorrect **$my_var = TRUE;**

HTML / CSS rules

Class names and IDs should be hyphenated and not use an underscore

Correct **class="my-class"** Incorrect **class="my_class"**

PHP Coding Standards Fixer

Ensure your code adheres to the project's standards effortlessly by utilizing PHP Coding Standards Fixer. The provided configuration allows for automatic code formatting. If your IDE doesn't already integrate with php-cs-fixer, run it as a standalone tool: Use the following command to apply code adjustments and align it with the project's Code Standard:

php tools/php-cs-fixer.phar fix -v

Integrating php-cs-fixer into your workflow ensures consistent code formatting, streamlining collaboration and maintaining a clean, standardized codebase.

Static Code Analysis

To preempt common coding mistakes, the code undergoes thorough analysis with the PHPStan code analyzer. Suppose your IDE does not have native integration with PHPStan. In that case, you can use it as a standalone tool:

Initiate the following command to analyze your code changes and identify any potential issues:

php tools/phpstan.phar

Leveraging PHPStan enhances code quality by detecting errors and inconsistencies early in the development process. This proactive approach aids in maintaining a robust and error-free codebase.

2. OPENCART SYSTEM LOADING FLOW

OpenCart is an e-commerce shopping cart application built on its own framework, which follows the MVCL (Model, View, Controller, Language) pattern. This pattern is also applied to each module in OpenCart. The controller manages the logic and fetches data from the model, then sends this data to the view for display.

Opencart Technical Architecture MVCL pattern

Opencart is based on this MVCL pattern. Let's see what the MVCL pattern is: The user requests the controller through URL

- The controller loads the language and sets the variable for any text used in the data.
- If data is needed from the database, the controller loads the model, asks for results and the model sends back results, then the controller sets results to data.
- All these data are sent to View which renders and shows the output.

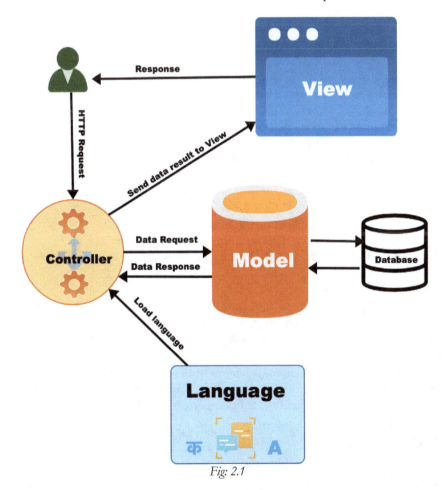

Fig: 2.1

The OpenCart structure is split into 2 separate applications. One is the catalog (store front) and admin (administration). The front and the admin are split into two folders and the shared library folder.

- admin - Administration Area
- catalog - Store Front
- system - Shared System Files

In the catalog and admin directories, you can see a tree structure of MVCL so whenever we create extensions or pages we follow these directory structures:

- **Controller** – The controller loads the language and sets the variable for any text used in the data. If data is needed from the database, the controller loads the model, asks for results and the model sends back results, then the controller sets results to data.
- **Model** – Database layer – All calls to the database are done. It is to structure DB calls so that all other files have access to the same DB queries.
- **View** – Presentation/Template/display layer – This is where the HTML and designing are done in the respective twig files.
- **Language** – Localization: This layer is to make the translation easy, variables and text are assigned and these folder files are translated to the respective language with the same variable name.

Opencart handles each request with a simple pattern for every incoming request that is interpreted by the routing URL "route=" and passed to the controller class matching the URL route part which returns Response objects. The controller is the only file in the MVC-L framework to be accessed by URL in Opencart. The controller is where all logic goes: it's where you interpret the request and create a response. It's that easy! Yes!

- Each request executes a front controller file
- The routing system determines which Controller class index method will be executed based on information from the request and routing URL you've passed.
- Returns the appropriate Response object.

Let's see some examples, webocreation.loc/index.php?route=account/login
Here "route=account/login", means that the controller to find in Opencart is
catalog/controller/**account/login.php** as there is no third one so by default the method is index().

http://webocreation.loc/index.php?route=account/return/add
Here "route=account/return/add", means that the controller to find in Opencart is
catalog/controller/**account/return.php and the method is add().**

- The controller has a namespace
  Example: namespace Opencart\Catalog\Controller\Account;, Here the Account is the folder. If you are creating your extension then the namespace can be something like this: namespace Opencart\Catalog\Controller\Extension**EXTENSIONNAME\EXTENSIONTYPE**;
- The controller class name can be the filename
- If your file name contains (_) underscore then no need to add in the controller name.
- The controller class must extend the parent class i.e.**\Opencart\System\Engine\Controller**
- The loader class is used to load the different components of OpenCart. Only the library classes can be auto-loaded upon Object Initialization.
  Example Controller load
  $this->load->controller('directory/filename');
  Example: *$this->load->controller('common/header');*
  Example Model load

$this->load->model('directory/filename');

Models can access directory in the code using:

$this->load->model('directory/filename');

Example view

$this->load->view('directory/filename', $data);

Example: *$this->load->view('account/login', $data)*

Example language load

$this->load->language('directory/filename');

Example: *$this->load->language('account/login');*

Let's check the code. Let's say the user requests the same URL
http://webocreation.loc/index.php?route=account/login
With route=account/login, the controller to process is controller/account/login.php's Login class and index method.

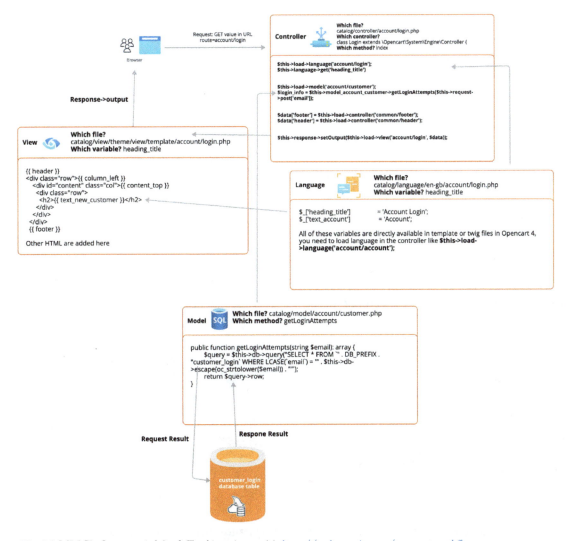

Fig: 2.2 MVCL Opencart 4 defined. For bigger image visit https://webocreation.com/opencart-mvcl-flow

We will delve into the steps OpenCart takes from the initial request to rendering the final output to the user.

23

1. Initial Request
   When a user accesses an OpenCart store, a request is made to the server. This request can be for any resource, such as a web page, image, or data. The request URL determines which resource is being requested and how the server should respond.

2. Index File: The starting point for OpenCart is the index.php file, located in both the root directory for the catalog (frontend) and the admin directory for the admin panel. This file acts as the entry point for all HTTP requests.
   // index.php or admin/index.php
   require_once('startup.php');

3. Startup File: The index.php file includes the startup.php file. This file sets up the necessary environment for OpenCart to run by initializing various components.
   // catalog/startup.php or admin/startup.php
   require_once(DIR_SYSTEM . 'framework.php');

4. Framework Initialization: The framework.php file is responsible for loading the essential system components. This includes loading configuration files, libraries, and defining constants.
   // system/framework.php
   require_once(DIR_SYSTEM . 'engine/registry.php');
   require_once(DIR_SYSTEM . 'engine/loader.php');
   require_once(DIR_SYSTEM . 'engine/controller.php');
   require_once(DIR_SYSTEM . 'engine/action.php');
   require_once(DIR_SYSTEM . 'engine/event.php');
   require_once(DIR_SYSTEM . 'library/config.php');
   require_once(DIR_SYSTEM . 'library/db.php');
   // Additional library files...

5. Registry Initialization: OpenCart uses a registry pattern to manage application-wide resources. The Registry class is instantiated to store objects like the configuration, database, loader, and other core components.
   $registry = new Registry();

6. Configuration Loading: Configuration settings are loaded from the database or configuration files into the registry. This includes site settings, database credentials, and other essential parameters.
   $config = new Config();
   $registry->set('config', $config);

7. Dependency Injection: Dependencies such as the database connection, loader, and session are created and injected into the registry.
   $loader = new Loader($registry);
   $registry->set('load', $loader);
   $db = new DB($config->get('db_driver'), $config->get('db_hostname'), $config->get('db_username'), $config->get('db_password'), $config->get('db_database'), $config->get('db_port'));
   $registry->set('db', $db);
   $session = new Session();
   $registry->set('session', $session);

8. Router: The router component determines which controller and action should handle the request. It parses the URL to decide the route.
   $router = new Router($registry);
   $router->addPreAction(new Action('startup/startup'));

// Load the default route
$action = new Action('common/home');
$action = $router->dispatch($action, new Action('error/not_found'));

9. Controller Execution: The router dispatches the request to the appropriate controller. Controllers are responsible for processing the request, interacting with models, and returning the response.
   $controller = new Controller($registry);
   $controller->index();

10. Model Interaction: Controllers interact with models to retrieve or manipulate data. Models handle the business logic and data transactions.
    $this->load->model('catalog/product');
    $products = $this->model_catalog_product->getProducts();

11. View Rendering: Once the controller has processed the request and obtained the necessary data, it passes this data to the view for rendering. Views are templates that generate the HTML output sent to the user's browser.
    $this->response->setOutput($this->load->view('common/home', $data));

12. Response: The final output is set in the response object, which sends the HTTP response back to the client.
    $response = new Response();
    $response->output();

Understanding the OpenCart system loading flow is crucial for developers who wish to customize and extend the platform. By knowing each step in the process, from the initial request to the final response, you can better troubleshoot issues, optimize performance, and develop more effective extensions and customizations. OpenCart's modular and organized architecture allows for a great deal of flexibility and control, making it a powerful tool for e-commerce development.

Describing files and folders of Opencart framework

Understanding the file and folder structure of OpenCart is crucial for anyone looking to customize or extend the platform. OpenCart's organized and modular architecture makes it easier to locate, modify, and manage various aspects of the store. Here's a detailed overview of the primary files and folders within the OpenCart framework.

Root Directory

The root directory of OpenCart contains essential files and directories that make up the core of the application. Key components include

config.php: This file contains the configuration settings for the catalog (front end) of the OpenCart store.

admin/config.php: Similar to the config.php file, but for the admin (back end) section.

index.php: The main entry point for the catalog. It initializes the framework and processes the incoming requests.

admin/index.php: The main entry point for the admin section, responsible for managing the backend operations.

.htaccess.txt: is a configuration file used on web servers running the Apache Web Server software where you rename the htaccess.txt to .htaccess. Mostly we use this for the SEO URL redirects in Opencart.

php.ini: is the configuration file for running applications. It is used to control variables, magic_quotes_gpc, register_globals, default_charset, memory_limit, max_execution_time, and many others. Shared hosting does not provide these facilities to change it but if you are hosting on Private servers then you can set it to use them.

Core Folders

admin/: The admin folder contains all the files and directories related to the administrative interface of OpenCart.

> **controller/**: Contains PHP files that handle the business logic for the admin interface.
>
> **language/**: Houses language files for translating the admin interface into different languages.
>
> **model/**: Contains models that interact with the database, handling data manipulation and retrieval for admin functions.
>
> **view/**: Contains the templates (usually in Twig format) and asset files like JavaScript, CSS, and images used in the admin interface.

catalog/: The catalog folder contains files and directories related to the front end of the OpenCart store.

> **controller/**: Houses controllers that manage the business logic for the storefront.
>
> **language/**: Contains language files for translating the front end into different languages.
>
> **model/**: Contains models that handle data interactions for the front end.
>
> **view/**: Contains the template files and assets for the storefront.

extension/: It contains all the extensions both default Opencart extensions and custom-installed extensions.

system/: The system folder contains core libraries and configuration files essential for the operation of OpenCart.

> **config/**: Contains configuration files.
>
> **library/**: Contains core libraries that provide essential functions and features to the framework.
>
> **engine/**: Contains core classes that drive the OpenCart framework, such as the registry, loader, and front controller.
>
> **helper/**: Contains helper functions that provide additional utilities to the core system.

image/: The image folder is used to store all the images for the store, including product images, category images, and other media assets.

> **cache/**: Stores cached images for faster loading.
>
> **catalog/**: Stores images related to the product catalog.

storage/: The storage folder is a secure location for sensitive files. It is usually moved outside the public web directory during the installation process for security purposes.

> **cache/**: Stores cached files to improve performance.
>
> **download/**: Contains downloadable files.
>
> **logs/**: Stores log files for debugging and tracking errors.
>
> **modification/**: Contains modified files generated by the modifications system.
>
> **session/**: Stores session files.
>
> **upload/**: Contains uploaded files.
>
> **marketplace:** All uploaded extensions are stored in the marketplace folder. The extensions are removed once deleted from the Installer.
>
> **vendor:** The vendor folder is an essential component of the OpenCart framework, enabling efficient management of third-party libraries through Composer.

install/: folder contains an Opencart.sql file which creates tables on the specified database and inserts demo data. Other files have codes that facilitate the installation of Opencart.

The OpenCart framework's file and folder structure is designed to be modular and organized, facilitating easy customization and extension. By understanding the purpose of each directory and key file, developers can efficiently navigate the platform, implement custom features, and maintain the store. This knowledge is essential for anyone looking to get the most out of OpenCart, whether for simple modifications or extensive development projects.

Opencart 4 Library Global Objects Methods

OpenCart 4 is built on a well-organized framework that uses various global objects and methods to manage its core functionalities. Understanding these objects and methods is essential for developers who wish to customize or extend OpenCart effectively.

An object has functions associated with it that are known as the object's methods. Here we show predefined objects that Opencart provided for which you don't need to create or initialize the objects, you can use it directly. So better to know them so that it helps in achieving DRY which means Don't Repeat Yourself.

Don't write code unless you should. Write code only what you need, if you missed these predefined objects' methods then you may repeat codes. Opencart has many predefined object methods that can be called in Controller and Model. Like in the admin section we can see predefined objects like config, log, event, load, request, response, DB, session, cache, URL, language, open-bay, document, customer, currency, tax, weight, length, cart, encryption, model_setting_event, the user. You can find most of the global objects defined at the system/library and go through all the files. Here are some examples, let's start with the system/library/db.php

DB (Database)

The DB class handles database interactions. It provides methods to execute queries and retrieve data from the database. You can look into system/library/db.php and can deep dive but overall, there are public methods that you can use in any extensions.

Methods:

> *query($sql): Executes a SQL query.*
>
> *escape($value): Escapes a value to prevent SQL injection.*
>
> *getLastId(): Returns the ID of the last inserted record.*
>
> *countAffected(): Returns the number of affected rows from the last query.*
>
> *isConnected(): Checks if a DB connection is active.*

In extensions, you can use like below:

> *$result = $this->db->query("SELECT * FROM " . DB_PREFIX . "product");*

Let's see an example of a database object:

The database object of Opencart is $this->db, which has the following methods. All SQL queries are run from the $this->db->query method which looks like below. For Select, replace, delete, and update we use it like this in Opencart and this returns three properties:

- Database Object of Opencart is $this->db
- Methods are:
  $this->**db**->escape($value) – mysql_real_escape_string() on the value passed
  $this->**db**->countAffected() – rows affected by an UPDATE query
  $this->**db**->getLastId() – last auto-increment id same as mysql_insert_id()
  $this->**db**->connected() – Pings a server connection, or tries to reconnect if the connection has gone down
  $this->**db**->query($sql)
- All SQL queries are run from $this->**db**->query method which looks like
  $query = $this->**db**->query(**"SELECT * FROM "** . *DB_PREFIX* . **"category WHERE**

```
$this->db->query("REPLACE INTO `" . DB_PREFIX . "category_path` SET ...);
$this->db->query("INSERT INTO `" . DB_PREFIX . "category_path` SET ...);
$this->db->query("DELETE FROM " . DB_PREFIX . "category WHERE ...);
$this->db->query("UPDATE " . DB_PREFIX . "category SET image = ...);
```

- $this->**db**->query method returns three properties:
  $result->**num_rows** = $query->**num_rows**; – gets the number of rows in a results
  $result->**row** = isset($data[0]) ? $data[0]: **array**(); – get the first row data
  $result->**rows** = $data; – get an array of row results

Customer

For customer objects, you see at system/library/cart/customer.php. You can see the namespace Cart which is like a directory, in Opencart 4 Customer is now under the "Cart" namespace. Customer object is instantiated as

$customer = **new** Cart\Customer($this->**registry**);

So, in the Customer class, there are private properties and public methods login, logout, islogged, getId, getFirstName, getLastName, getGroupId, getEmail, getTelephone, getNewsletter, isSafe, isCommenter, getAddressId, getBalance, and getRewardPoints. These public methods are available in the Controller and Model class of extensions which we already showed for DB objects and it's similar for other objects as well. You can see the login method of the customer object used in catalog/controller/account/login.php, You can see the $this->**customer**->login validate() method. Like this, we use the predefined method wherever we need it.

This login method is used to provide the authentication for the customer section of Opencart. Customer session is activated for customer_id, first name, last name, customer_group_id, email, telephone, newsletter, and address_id is assigned.

If you check the customer object without login all values assigned are null,

echo "<pre>";
var_dump($this->**customer**);
echo "</pre>";

Once you log in values, you can see these values. Now in code, you can get those values through public methods provided by the customer object to get the first name we have the getFirstName method:

echo "<pre>";
print_r($this->**customer**->getFirstName());
echo "</pre>";

If you are confused about how to get the class methods name then PHP has get_class_method function:

echo "<pre>";
$class_methods = *get_class_methods*($this->**config**);
print_r($class_methods);
echo "</pre>";

With this logout method is used to unset the customer session and assign an empty value.

Methods:

login(string $email, string $password, bool $override = false): method of customer object is used to check whether customer_id is active or not.

logout(): Logout

isLogged(): Checked if the customer is logged in or not

getId(): Get the id of the active customer

getFirstName(): It returns an active customer First name

getLastName(): It returns an active customer Last name

getGroupId(): It returns an active ground id of the customer

getEmail(): It returns active customer email

getTelephone(): It returns an active customer telephone number

getNewsletter(): It returns if the customer is subscribed to newsletter

isSafe(): It returns if the safe is active in customer

isCommenter(): It returns if the commenter is active in customer

getAddressId(): It returns the default address of the customer

getBalance(): It returns the balance of the customer

getRewardPoints(): It returns the reward points of the customer

Registry

The Registry class is a core component in OpenCart that acts as a storage for global objects. It ensures that different parts of the application can share common resources without redundant initialization. If you look in the system/framework.php, you will see lots of *$registry->set*. For developers, it is rarely used while developing the extensions but if you want to advance and customize the main framework flow, this could be very useful.

Methods:

set($key, $value): Stores an object or value in the registry.

get($key): Retrieves an object or value from the registry.

has($key): Checks if an object or value is set in the registry.

$registry = new Registry();

$registry->set('config', new Config());

$config = $registry->get('config');

Config

The Config class manages configuration settings for the application. It provides methods to set and get configuration values.

Methods:

load($filename): Loads a configuration file.

get($key): Retrieves a configuration value.

set($key, $value): Sets a configuration value.

$config = new Config();

$config->set('config_url', 'https://example.com');

echo $config->get('config_url');

For developers, this is very useful, you can get all the settings values by doing $this->config->get('thevariablename'). If you have extensions that have setting page and form values that need to be saved then you can use $this->config->set. In admin >> System >> Settings >> Edit Store >> Option tab >> Products >> Default items per page. You can access that value by doing $this->config->get('config_pagination')). In this way, you can access all get and set values in any extensions from the oc_settings database table with $this->config->get and $this->config->set.

Loader

The Loader class is responsible for loading models, views, and language files. It ensures that these components are properly instantiated and available for use.
Methods:

> *model($route): Loads a model.*
>
> *view($route, $data = array()): Loads a view and returns the rendered output.*
>
> *language($route): Loads a language file.*
>
> *$loader = new Loader($registry);*
>
> *$loader->model('catalog/product');*
>
> *$this->load->view('common/header', $data);*
>
> *$this->load->language('common/footer');*

Language

The Language class manages translations and language files. It provides methods to load language files and retrieve translated strings.
Methods:

> *load($filename): Loads a language file.*
>
> *get($key): Retrieves a translated string.*
>
> *$language = new Language('en-gb');*
>
> *$language->load('common/footer');*
>
> *echo $language->get('text_footer');*

Url

The Url class is responsible for generating URLs for different parts of the application. It ensures that URLs are correctly formatted and SEO-friendly.
Methods:

> *link($route, $args = '', $secure = false): Generates a URL for a given route and parameters.*
>
> *$url = new Url('https://example.com', 'https://secure.example.com');*
>
> *echo $url->link('product/product', 'product_id=42');*

Document

The Document class manages the document properties for the response, such as the title, meta tags, stylesheets, and scripts.
Methods:

> *setTitle($title): Sets the document title.*
>
> *addLink($href, $rel): Adds a link tag to the document.*
>
> *addScript($script): Adds a script tag to the document.*
>
> *addStyle($style): Adds a style tag to the document.*

In extension you can use like below:

> *$this->document->setTitle($this->language->get('heading_title'));*
>
> *$this->document->addScript('catalog/view/javascript/common.js');*
>
> *$this->document->addStyle('catalog/view/theme/default/stylesheet/stylesheet.css');*

Response

The Response class handles the HTTP response sent to the client. It manages the headers, output, and status codes.
Methods:

setOutput($output): Sets the output content for the response.

addHeader($header): Adds a header to the response.

setCompression($level): Sets the compression level for the response.

output(): Sends the response to the client.

$response = new Response();

$response->setOutput($output);

$response->addHeader('Content-Type: text/html; charset=utf-8');

$response->output();

Request

The Request class encapsulates the HTTP request data, such as GET, POST, and COOKIE variables. It provides methods to retrieve this data safely.

Methods:

get($key): Retrieves a value from the GET variables.

post($key): Retrieves a value from the POST variables.

cookie($key): Retrieves a value from the COOKIE variables.

server($key): Retrieves a value from the SERVER variables.

$request = new Request();

$product_id = $request->get['product_id'];

$username = $request->post['username'];

The global objects and methods in OpenCart 4 provide a robust framework for building and extending an e-commerce application. By understanding how to utilize these objects, developers can efficiently manage configurations, load necessary components, interact with the database, handle requests and responses, and ensure the application runs smoothly. This knowledge is essential for customizing OpenCart to meet specific business needs and creating a seamless shopping experience for users.

Cart, you can see the system/library/cart/cart.php where you can see the public methods that can be accessed from your modules. You can see here the getProducts method, add method, remove method, and so on.

Namespace in Opencart

- A namespace is like a directory and by adding 'namespace', Affiliate is now under 'Cart'.
- To use 'Affiliate', we call or instantiate as new Cart\Affiliate()
- Adding a 'namespace' to a class is like organizing files from one directory into a bunch of sub-directories.
- The use statement lets us call class by a nickname.

Affiliate

- $this->affiliate->login($email, $password);
  You can find code used at *catalog/controller/affiliate/login.php validate()* method.
  Affiliate *login* script at *system/library/cart/affiliate.php* is used to provide the authentication for the Affiliate section of Opencart. Affiliate session is activated for affiliate_id, firstname, lastname, email, telephone, fax, and code.
- $this->affiliate->logout()
  You can find the code used at catalog/controller/affiliate/logout.php index() method.
  Affiliate logout script at system/library/cart/affiliate.php is used to unset the affiliate session and assign empty value to affiliate_id, firstname, lastname, email, telephone, and fax of Affiliate. This

Affiliate is logged out.

- $this->affiliate->isLogged()
  You can find the code used at *catalog/controller/affiliate/account.php index()* method.
  Affiliate *isLogged* script at *system/library/cart/affiliate.php* is used to check whether affiliate_id is active or not.
- $this->affiliate->getId()
  You can find code used at *catalog/model/affiliate/affiliate.php editAffiliate($data)* method.
  The affiliate *getId* script at *system/library/cart/affiliate.php* is used to return active affiliate_id.
- $this->affiliate->getFirstName()
  You can find code used at *catalog/controller/affiliate/login.php* index*()* method.
  The affiliate getFirstName script at *system/library/cart/affiliate.php* is used to return the active affiliate's first name.
- $this->affiliate->getLastName()
  You can find code used at *catalog/controller/affiliate/login.php* index*()* method.
  The affiliate getLastName script at *system/library/cart/affiliate.php* is used to return an active affiliate's last name.
- $this->affiliate->getEmail()
  You can find code used at *catalog/controller/affiliate/edit.php* validate() method.
  Affiliate getEmail script at *system/library/cart/affiliate.php* is used to return active affiliate email.
- $this->affiliate->getTelephone()
  Not used in Opencart but you can use it J.
  Affiliate getTelephone script at *system/library/cart/affiliate.php* is used to return active affiliate Telephone numbers.
- $this->affiliate->getCode()
  You can find code used at catalog/controller/affiliate/tracking.php index() method.
  Affiliate getCode script at *system/library/cart/affiliate.php* is used to return active affiliate tracking code which is used to track referrals.
- $this->affiliate->getFax()
  Not used in Opencart but you can use it J.
  Affiliate getFax script at *system/library/cart/affiliate.php* is used to return the active affiliate Fax number.

Other Global Methods

- Cache
- Cart
- Currency
- Customer
- Length
- Tax
- User
- Weight
- Config
- DB
- Document
- Image
- Language
- Log
- Mail
- Request
- Response
- Session
- Template
- URL

So, you get where to see the Opencart library's predefined objects' methods which you can use in our Model and controller classes. Keep digging.

$this reference in the controller

Go to admin/controller/extension/module account.php and var_dump the $this,

```
echo "<pre>";
var_dump($this);
echo "</pre>";
exit();
```

$this is a reference to the calling object, usually the object to which the method belongs. You can see the protected modifier registry which has config, log, event, load, request, response, etc.

Now let's take the config object:

```
echo "<pre>";
$class_methods = get_class_methods($this->config);
print_r($class_methods);
echo "</pre>";
```

Now, you can see the list of methods that you can use in your config object.

Let's see the parameters that you can use in the get and set methods:
```
echo"<pre>";
var_dump($this->config);
echo "</pre>";
exit();
```

Now let's say we want the site URL then we can easily get it as following

```
print_r($this->config->get('site_url'));
exit();
```

In this way, you can keep on using other objects and methods that Opencart 4 provides by default.

3. UNDERSTAND OPENCART DATABASE

We need to know about the database and global methods of Opencart then it will be easier to understand the Opencart code flow. So, in this chapter, we will go through the Opencart database. Things to consider while creating database Opencart Guide

- Opencart supports multi-store
- It supports multi-language
- Multiple Layouts
- You can see the database prefix at config.php, and see the constant DB_PREFIX, by default *oc_* is the database prefix
- If you are creating the table then better to make 4 tables, one which will contain language-specific contents here oc_information_description, another is non-language specific oc_information and another which joins with the store and last one which joins to the layout.

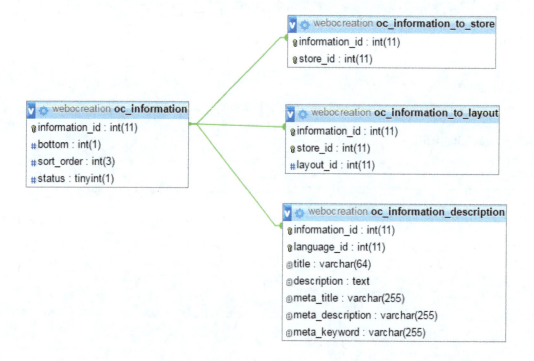

Fig: 3.1

Create a custom table schema in Opencart

If you are going to create a custom table in Opencart then you have to think of four tables. One table contains non-language-specific like in the above image oc_information, another table is language-specific in the above image oc_information_description, another table shows the relationship between store and data in the above image oc_information_to_store and the last one shows the relationship between layout and data.

So if you want to create a custom table that contains testimonials then your table schema will be like in the image:

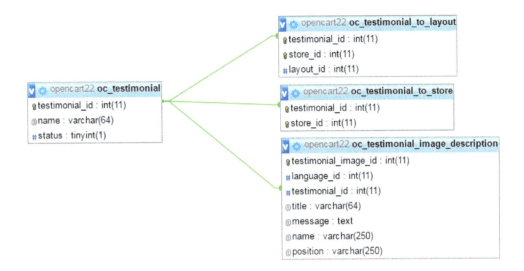

Fig: 3.2

Model Code flow example

- **Create a model file:** admin>>model>>catalog>>information.php
- **Create a class as per the folder and file structure:**
  class **Information** extends **\Opencart\System\Engine\Model**
- **Create a Method inside the class:** public function addInformation($data)
- **In Controller, first load the model then call the method:**
  $this->load->model('catalog/information');
  $this->model_catalog_information->addInformation($this->request->post);

Install method to run the create SQL and insert SQL for default values

In the extension controller you can write the install method, which gets auto called after clicking the install button. An example used in Bestseller is like below and you can add the same install function for your custom extension.

```
public function install(): void {
    if ($this->user->hasPermission('modify', 'extension/Opencart/module/bestseller')) {
        $this->load->model('extension/Opencart/module/bestseller');
        $this->model_extension_Opencart_module_bestseller->install();
    }
}
```

In the model, the install method creates the product_bestseller database table. Here is the example query:

```
public function install(): void {
    $this->db->query("CREATE TABLE IF NOT EXISTS `". DB_PREFIX . "product_bestseller` (
        `product_id` int(11) NOT NULL,
        `total` int(11) NOT NULL,
        PRIMARY KEY (`product_id`)
    ) ENGINE=InnoDB DEFAULT CHARSET=utf8mb4 COLLATE=utf8mb4_general_ci");
}
```

Uninstall the method to run the drop SQL

Like the install method, the uninstall method also autorun after the uninstall button is clicked.

```
public function uninstall(): void {
    if ($this->user->hasPermission('modify', 'extension/Opencart/module/bestseller')) {
        $this->load->model('extension/Opencart/module/bestseller');
        $this->model_extension_Opencart_module_bestseller->uninstall();
    }
}
```

Here is the query to drop the product_bestseller table:

```
public function uninstall(): void { $this->db->query("DROP TABLE IF EXISTS `" . DB_PREFIX . "product_bestseller`");}
```

Some example SQL queries:

Get products of specific dates or between dates

```
$query = $this->db->query("SELECT DISTINCT * FROM `". DB_PREFIX . "product` `p` LEFT JOIN `".
DB_PREFIX . "product_description` `pd` ON (`p`.`product_id` = `pd`.`product_id`) WHERE `p`.`product_id` = '".
(int)$product_id . "' AND `pd`.`language_id` = '". (int)$this->config->get('config_language_id') . "' AND
`p`.`date_added` BETWEEN 2022-02-03  AND 2024-02-03");
```

Merge two Opencart databases into one

We had a project to merge two Opencart databases into one, we are not going into details but the basic flow we set is we make a connection to two databases at system/framework.php like below:

```
128    // Database
129    if ($config->get('db_autostart')) {
130        $db = new \Opencart\System\Library\DB($config->get('db_engine'), $config->get('db_hostname'), $config->get('db_username'), $config->get
           ('db_password'), $config->get('db_database'), $config->get('db_port'), $config->get('db_ssl_key'), $config->get('db_ssl_cert'), $config->get
           ('db_ssl_ca'));
131        $registry->set('db', $db);
132
133        $db2 = new \Opencart\System\Library\DB($config->get('db_engine'), "DB2_HOSTURL", "DB2_USERNAME", "DB2_PASSWORD, $config->get('db_database'),
           $config->get('db_port'), $config->get('db_ssl_key'), $config->get('db_ssl_cert'), $config->get('db_ssl_ca'));
134        $registry->set('db2', $db2);
135    }
```

```
$db2 = new \Opencart\System\Library\DB($config->get('db_engine'), "DB2_HOSTURL",
"DB2_USERNAME", "DB2_PASSWORD, $config->get('db_database'), $config->get('db_port'), $config-
>get('db_ssl_key'), $config->get('db_ssl_cert'), $config->get('db_ssl_ca'));
$registry->set('db2', $db2);
```

Change as per your database connections information.

Now in your modules, you can call the second database like *$this->db2->query("SQL")*. One customer example is like this, here we show you only the partial code:

```
//all customer
$cquery = $this->db2->query("SELECT * FROM `" . DB_PREFIX2 . "customer` ORDER BY `customer_id` ASC LIMIT " . (int)
$start . "," . (int) $limit);
if ($cquery->num_rows) {
    foreach ($cquery->rows as $cdatas) {

        $cquery = $this->db->query("SELECT * FROM `oc_customer` where email='" . $cdatas['email'] . "'");
        if ($cquery->row) {
            //Update Customer if needed
        } else {
            //customer
            $this->db->query("INSERT INTO `" . DB_PREFIX . "customer` SET `language_id` = '" . $cdatas
            ['language_id'] . "', `store_id` = '" . (int) $cdatas['store_id'] . "', `customer_group_id` = '" .
```

Fig: 3.3

Database Schema Relationship

Here is an example of an information tables schema relationship, where you can show information tables with their relationship.

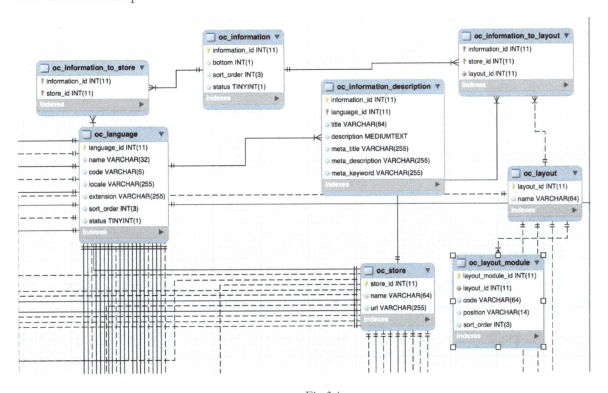

Fig: 3.4

You can get the whole Opencart Schema diagram from the Opencart GitHub docs folder:

https://github.com/Opencart/Opencart/blob/master/docs/database/Opencart%20-%20DB%20Schema.pdf

Mysql Workbench file: *https://github.com/Opencart/Opencart/blob/master/docs/database/Opencart%20-%20DB%20Schema.mwb*

4. OPENCART EVENT SYSTEM

Opencart Events are hooks that developers can attach custom code to, allowing them to execute specific actions at different points in the application's lifecycle. Events can be triggered by various actions within the Opencart system, such as user authentication, order creation, product editing, email being sent, and more.

Event Types

Pre-Events: Triggered before a specific action occurs. For example, a pre-event can be triggered before an order is saved, allowing developers to perform custom actions like validating order data.

Post-Events: Triggered after a specific action occurs. For example, a post-event can be triggered after a product is edited, allowing developers to perform custom actions like updating related data.

Using Opencart Events:

To use Opencart events, developers need to create an event listener, which is a function or method that responds to a specific event. An event completes the tasks that a controller, a model, a theme override, a language, and a config need to be achieved in the back end of the store. Upon startup, the Engine automatically registers triggers, and actions, and sorts orders in both the admin/controller/startup/event.php and catalog/controller/startup/event.php files.

Event listeners are registered using the addEvent method from the Event class. The method takes three parameters: the event name, the class/method to be executed, and the priority of the listener. Example Code:

```
// In your custom extension, add this code to the controller
$this->event->addEvent('catalog/controller/product/product/after', 'extension/event/custom_event/afterProductView');
// Define the event listener in your custom event class
class ControllerExtensionEventCustomEvent extends Controller {
    public function afterProductView(&$route, &$data, &$output) {
        // Custom code to execute after a product view
        // Example: modify the product data before it's rendered
        $data['custom_text'] = 'This is a custom message after product view.';
    }
```

}

Registering Events:

Events can be registered in an extension's install method or directly in the controller if needed.

It's important to unregister events in the extensions and uninstall the method to avoid any unwanted behavior after removing the extension.

Using Events for Customization:

Developers can use Opencart events to customize and extend the platform in various ways, such as

- Adding custom logic to product pages, checkout processes, or other areas of the platform.
- Modifying data before it's displayed to the user.
- Integrating with third-party services or APIs.

For developers, add event code, description, trigger, and action in the database. The action is the method that does what you want. A trigger is the path that you want for the existing Opencart controller and methods.

event_id	code	description	trigger	action	status	sort_order
1	activity_customer_add		catalog/model/account/customer/addCustomer/after	event/activity.addCustomer	1	1
2	activity_customer_edit		catalog/model/account/customer/editCustomer/after	event/activity.editCustomer	1	1
3	activity_customer_password		catalog/model/account/customer/editPassword/after	event/activity.editPassword	1	1
4	activity_customer_forgotten		catalog/model/account/customer/editCode/after	event/activity.forgotten	1	1
5	activity_customer_login		catalog/model/account/customer/deleteLoginAttempts/after	event/activity.login	1	1

Fig: 4.1

You can see all the events at >> Admin >> Extensions >> Events

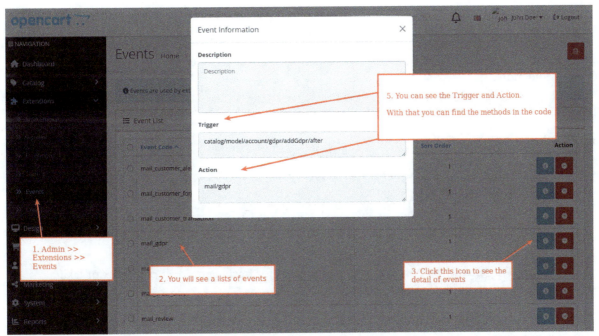

Fig: 4.2

List of Events

Catalog and admin events, here are the lists of Catalog events for different functionalities.

Language events

Opencart's language events system is an important part of managing and customizing language-related aspects of the platform. Language events allow developers to add, modify, or manipulate language files and translations within the Opencart application. This is crucial for providing multilingual support and customizing text displayed to users.

view/*/before	Dump all the language vars into the template.
controller/*/before	Before the controller loads store all current loaded language data
controller/*/after	After the controller, load restores old language data

Activity events

Opencart's activity events system allows developers to monitor and respond to user activities and other important events within the platform. These events are useful for tracking user actions, generating logs, and performing custom operations based on specific activities. This system enhances the ability to understand user behavior, provide better support, and maintain the platform effectively.

Here's an overview of Opencart activity events and how you can use them:

Understanding Activity Events:

Activity events in Opencart track significant actions performed by users, such as login, logout, product views, purchases, and more.

These events enable developers to create custom responses and logs based on specific user activities.

Common Activity Events:

customer_login: Triggered when a customer logs in. This event is useful for monitoring login activity or taking specific actions upon login.

customer_logout: Triggered when a customer logs out. You can use this event to perform cleanup operations or logging.

product_viewed: Triggered when a product is viewed. Useful for tracking product popularity or taking custom actions based on product views.

order_added: Triggered when a new order is added. This event can be used to log order information or trigger post-order processes.

customer_register: Triggered when a customer registers a new account. Useful for sending welcome emails or performing other onboarding activities.

Creating Activity Event Listeners:

To use activity events, create event listeners that respond to specific events of interest.

Register event listeners in your extension's controller using the addEvent method from the Event class.

```
// Registering an activity event listener in your controller
$this->event->addEvent('customer_login', 'extension/event/activity/onCustomerLogin');
// Define the event listener method in your custom event class
class ControllerExtensionEventActivity extends Controller {
    public function onCustomerLogin(&$route, &$args, &$output) {
        // Custom code to execute when a customer logs in
        // For example, log the customer login event
        $this->log->write('Customer logged in: ' . $args['customer_id']);
    }
}
```

Here are default Opencart Activity Event list:

catalog/model/account/customer/addCustomer/after	
catalog/model/account/customer/editCustomer/after	
catalog/model/account/customer/editPassword/after	
catalog/model/account/customer/deleteLoginAttempts/after	
catalog/model/account/customer/editCode/after	
catalog/model/account/customer/addTransaction/after	
catalog/model/account/affiliate/addAffiliate/after	
catalog/model/account/affiliate/editAffiliate/after	
catalog/model/account/address/addAddress/after	
catalog/model/account/address/editAddress/after	
catalog/model/account/address/deleteAddress/after	
catalog/model/account/returns/addReturn/after	
catalog/model/checkout/order/addHistory/before	

Statistics events

catalog/model/catalog/review/addReview/after	
catalog/model/account/returns/addReturn/after	
catalog/model/checkout/order/addHistory/before	

Theme event

Opencart's theme events system allows developers to customize and extend the behavior of themes within the platform. By using theme events, you can modify how themes render content, alter page elements, and integrate custom logic to achieve a unique look and feel for your store.

Here's an overview of Opencart theme events and how you can utilize them:

Understanding Theme Events:

Theme events are hooks that allow you to customize the rendering of pages and elements in your Opencart theme. These events are triggered during different stages of the rendering process and provide opportunities to manipulate the data or layout before it's displayed to users.

Common Theme Events:

view/*/before: Triggered before rendering a view file in a specific directory, such as catalog/view/theme/[theme_name].

view/*/after: Triggered after rendering a view file in a specific directory.

template/*/before: Triggered before rendering a template file in a specific directory, such as catalog/view/theme/[theme_name]/template.

template/*/after: Triggered after rendering a template file in a specific directory.

Creating Theme Event Listeners:

To use Theme events, you need to create event listeners that respond to the specific events you want to customize.

Register event listeners in your extension's controller using the addEvent method from the Event class.

```
// Registering a theme event listener in your controller
$this->event->addEvent('view/common/header/before', 'extension/event/theme/customizeHeader');
// Define the event listener method in your custom event class
class ControllerExtensionEventThemeCustomizeHeader extends Controller {
    public function customizeHeader(&$route, &$data, &$output) {
        // Custom code to modify the header before rendering
        $data['custom_message'] = 'Welcome to our store!';
    }
}
```

Here are lists of Opencart theme events:

view/*/before	
view/*/after	
template/*/before	
template/*/after	

Here is the main code for the catalog that controls the theme events:
upload/catalog/controller/event/theme.php

```php
class Theme extends \Opencart\System\Engine\Controller {
    public function index(string &$route, array &$args, string &$code): void {
        // If there is a theme override we should get it
        $this->load->model('design/theme');
        $theme_info = $this->model_design_theme->getTheme($route, $this->config->get('config_theme'));
        if ($theme_info) {
            $code = html_entity_decode($theme_info['code'], ENT_QUOTES, 'UTF-8');
        }
    }
}
```

Let's say you want to override all the common/header while creating your theme, then you can use something like below, we named the theme as **webocreation**:

```php
<?php
namespace Opencart\Catalog\Controller\Extension\webocreation\Startup;
class Standard extends \Opencart\System\Engine\Controller
{
    public function index(): void
    {
        if ($this->config->get('webocreation_status')) {
            $this->event->register('view/*/before', new
\Opencart\System\Engine\Action('extension/webocreation/startup/standard|event'));
        }
    }
    public function event(string &$route, array &$args, mixed &$output): void
    {
        $override = [
            'common/header',
        ];
        if (in_array($route, $override)) {
```

```
        $route = 'extension/webocreation/' . $route;
      }
    }
  }
```

Admin Currency Events

model/setting/setting/editSetting	
model/localisation/currency/addCurrency	
model/localisation/currency/editCurrency	

Admin Statistics Events

admin/model/catalog/review/addReview/after	
admin/model/catalog/review/deleteReview/after	
admin/model/sale/returns/addReturn/after	
admin/model/sale/returns/deleteReturn/after	

Translation Event

Opencart's translation events system allows developers to customize and extend the language and translation aspects of the platform. By using translation events, you can modify or extend the existing translations, add new language strings, and customize language files to achieve a more personalized or localized experience for your store. Here is the main code that you can find at upload/catalog/controller/event/translation.php and upload/admin/controller/design/translation.php

```
class Translation extends \Opencart\System\Engine\Controller {
  public function index(string &$route, string &$prefix): void {
    $this->load->model('design/translation');
    $results = $this->model_design_translation->getTranslations($route);
    foreach ($results as $result) {
      if (!$prefix) {
        $this->language->set($result['key'], html_entity_decode($result['value'], ENT_QUOTES, 'UTF-8'));
      } else {
        $this->language->set($prefix . '_' . $result['key'], html_entity_decode($result['value'], ENT_QUOTES, 'UTF-8'));
      }
    }
  }
}
```

Admin Language Events

view/*/before	
controller/*/before	
controller/*/after	

Testing Output with Opencart Events

By default, in the system/config/catalog.php file, the debug key and value are commented out at the bottom because they should only be active for debugging purposes. Remove the comment of the code like below:

```
// Action Events
$_['action_event'] = [
        'controller/*/before' => [
                0 => 'event/language.before',
                1 => 'event/debug.before'
        ],
        'controller/*/after' => [
                0 => 'event/language.after',
                2 => 'event/debug.after'
        ],
        'view/*/before' => [
                500 => 'event/theme',
                998 => 'event/language'
        ],
        'language/*/after' => [
                0 => 'startup/language.after',
                1 => 'event/translation'
        ]
];
```

After enabling debugging, you can test the code within the catalog/controller/event/debug.php file. You see the after and before methods. Here is an example of an after-test to find all the routes used on the page.

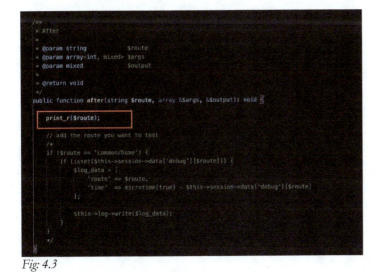

Fig: 4.3

After testing, it is essential to undo the debugging changes by commenting out the debugs line in the system/config/catalog.php file.

Challenges

- **Performance Impact:** Every event adds a layer of processing, which can slightly impact page load times, especially with numerous event handlers. Monitor performance and prioritize essential events to avoid noticeable slowdowns.
- **Debugging Complexity:** Debugging problems within event handlers can be more challenging than traditional code because they may be triggered from different locations. Employ proper logging and testing practices to identify and resolve issues effectively.
- **Security Risks:** Improper event handler implementation might introduce security vulnerabilities. Always validate and sanitize user input within event handlers to prevent potential security risks.
- **Maintenance burden:** As your store and codebase grow, managing numerous event handlers can become complex. Organize your events and handlers logically, document their purpose, and update them regularly to maintain code clarity and avoid conflicts.
- **Version compatibility:** While events strive for backward compatibility, updates to core files or other extensions might break event handlers. Thoroughly test your events after updates to ensure continued functionality.

Best Practices while using Opencart Events:

- **Use events judiciously:** Don't overuse events for simple tasks that can be handled efficiently within core files. Reserve events for extending functionality beyond core capabilities.
- **Write clean and efficient code:** Optimize your event handlers for performance and avoid unnecessary processing.
- **Test thoroughly:** Test your event handlers under various scenarios, including edge cases and potential conflicts with other extensions.
- **Document your work:** Document the purpose and logic of your event handlers to facilitate future maintenance and collaboration.
- **Stay updated:** Monitor changes in Opencart and event-related functionality to adapt your code when necessary.

5. OPENCART 4 OCMOD

In this Chapter, we cover Opencart 4 OCMOD and show how to start coding in OCMOD to change the files and extend the functionalities of Opencart.

OCMOD is a system that allows store owners to be able to modify their store by uploading a compressed file that contains XML, SQL, and PHP files. If an OCMOD is developed correctly it can modify a user's Opencart store without changing any of the core files, This means that if a modification is removed none of the original Opencart files need to be restored or fixed.

Here we will show the flows that happened when someone uploads the ***.ocmod.zip file, then create a test.ocmod..xml file to show the module link in the left column and give you details of Ocmod documentation in Opencart 4.

Files and folder structure OCMOD extension

All the OCMOD XML should be inside the OCMOD folder. Here in the example we are creating the webocreation_admin_menu extension folder inside it are the install.json and OCMOD folders. In the OCMOD folder, we add the XML file, the XML file name should be the same as the code. Here the file name is webocreation_admin_menu.ocmod.xml and in the XML the code is
<code>webocreation_admin_menu</code>

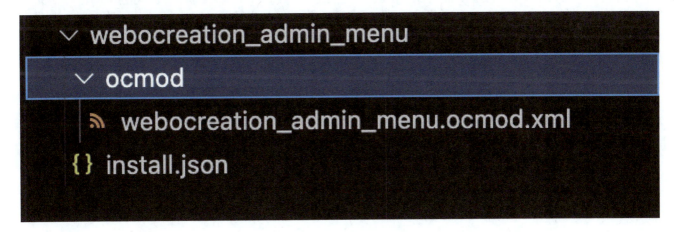

Fig: 5.1

The Flow of OCMOD

Upload of extension with OCMOD

As per the core code when you upload the ***.ocmod.zip folder from Extensions >> Installer, the following things will happen:

1. Check if the user has permission. You will get an error like:
   "Warning: You do not have permission to modify modifications!"
2. Check if there is an installed temporary folder zip already there. If it finds the file and the file created time is less than 5 seconds then it tries to unlink or remove the file, if it cannot remove the file then it throws an error saying:
   "Extension installation taking place please wait a few seconds before trying to install!"
3. It checks whether the filename is between 3 and 128 characters or not. If not it will show an error like:
   'Filename must be between 3 and 128 characters!';
4. It checks whether the uploaded zip file ends with .ocmod.zip
5. It checks if there are any other file uploading errors, UPLOAD_ERR_OK: Value: 0; There is no error, and the file uploaded with success. If there is any error it will show an error like:
   "File could not be uploaded!"
6. If everything is good then it creates a .tmp file and performs the function move_uploaded_file.
7. Then it checks if the module file already exists or if the module code is already in the database or not. If it exists, it throws the following error:
   'Extension already installed!'
8. If all the above are good then it validates if the file can be opened and there is install.json that can be read. If it cannot find the install.json, then it throws the following error:
   'Warning: Could not find install.json!'
9. If there is an issue with unzipping the ocmod.zip file then it throws the following error:
   'Zip file could not be opened!'
10. If everything is fine then it gets all the info from the install.json. It gets a name, description, code, version, author, and link
11. Then finally it adds the extension details to the database table *oc_extension_install*. The query ran is below:
    $this->db->query("INSERT INTO `" . DB_PREFIX . "extension_install` SET `extension_id` = '" . (int)$data['extension_id'] . "', `extension_download_id` = '" . (int)$data['extension_download_id'] . "', `name` = '" . $this->db->escape($data['name']) . "', `description` = '" . $this->db->escape($data['description']) . "', `code` = '" . $this->db->escape($data['code']) . "', `version` = '" . $this->db->escape($data['version']) . "', `author` = '" . $this->db->escape($data['author']) . "', `link` = '" . $this->db->escape($data['link']) . "', `status` = '0', `date_added` = NOW()");
    As you see the status is still 0. Now the file is uploaded and extension info is added to the database. With this, the upload is completed.

Installation of OCMOD extension

After the extension is uploaded, you will see those extensions listed at Extensions >> Installer. You will see something like the following:

Installed Extensions

Extension Name ∧	Version	Date Added	Action
OpenCart Default Extensions	1.0	29/08/2020	
OpenCart Language Example	1.0	28/04/2024	
OpenCart OCMOD Example	1.0	28/04/2024	
OpenCart Payment Example	1.0	28/04/2024	
OpenCart Theme Example	1.0	28/04/2024	

Fig: 5.2

Now, we are showing the flows that happened when you click the Install button for the Opencart OCMOD Example extension.

1. Check if the user has permission. You will get an error like:
   "Warning: You do not have permission to modify modifications!"
2. Then it gets the detail of the extension from *oc_extension_install* database table
3. It makes sure the file exists in the storage folder >> Marketplace. If the file is not found then it shows an error like:
   'Install file %s could not be found!';
4. If there are no errors, then it starts unzipping the ***.ocmod.zip and if it cannot unzip the ocmod.zip file then it shows an error like:
   "Zip file could not be opened!"
5. After unzipping it checks if any of the files already exist. It only extracts the contents of the upload folder. If there are images, it copies the images, then it stores the path differently for vendor folders.
6. It checks if the path is not a directory and checks if there is no existing file, then it puts the file and adds the path in the oc_extension_path database table.
7. It enables the module by updating the status of the module at oc_extension_install database table
8. It adds the XML code in the oc_modification table

modification_id	extension_install_id	name	description	code	author	version	link	xml	status
2	6	Webocreation Admin Menu	Add a Module link in top menu item in the Admin se...	webocreation_admin_menu	Webocreation	1.0	https://webocreation.com	<?xml version="1.0" encoding="utf-8"?> <modificat...	1

Fig: 5.3

9. Finally, it gives the success message.
10. Go to Extensions and Modifications and Install the extension by clicking the green install button

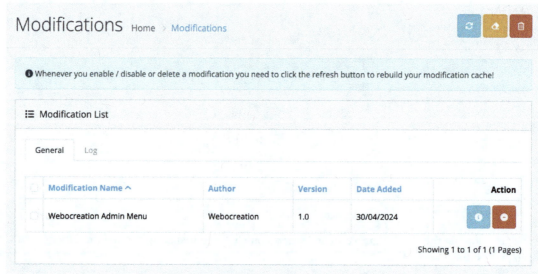

Fig: 5.4

11. Click the Clear icon and you will see the applied OCMOD

OCMOD developer tips

- Extension folder needs OCMOD folder
- File name except ocmod.zip and <code> value should be the same.
- While zipping the folder zip the install.json and ocmod/ folder, not the folder.
- Testing is hard for OCMOD changes if you have to change in XML, zip, upload from the installer, and clear in modifications. So the tip for developers is they can upload the extension and enable it, then make changes in the extension code from the extension folder and you don't need to zip and upload again and again, you can just clear the cache in modifications and you can check the changes, and once you are satisfied you can copy and make the extension and upload it.
- oc_modification, oc_extension_install, and oc_extension_path are the three database tables that are touched after the OCMOD extension is uploaded and installed.

Example OCMOD code

In the install.xml it should be something like where the ****** is your custom thing.

```xml
<?xml version="1.0" encoding="utf-8"?>
<modification>
    <name>******</name>
    <version>******</version>
    <author>******</author>
    <link>******</link>
    <code>******</code>
    <description>******</description>
    <file path="******">
        <operation>
            <search><![CDATA[ ****** ]]></search>
            <add position="******"><![CDATA[******]]></add>
        </operation>
    </file>
</modification>
```

Don't forget <code>, although it is not mentioned in the Modification system documentation https://github.com/Opencart/Opencart/wiki/Modification-System. You can use multiple file operations. There are two operations search and add. With the add operation, you can replace, add before, or add after by adding in the position.

```
<file path="">
  <operation>
    <search><![CDATA[]]></search>
    <add position=""><![CDATA[]]></add>
  </operation>
</file>
```

Controller OCMOD code example

```
<file path="admin/controller/catalog/attribute.php">
  <operation>
    <search>
      <![CDATA[Opencart\Admin\Controller\Catalog;]]>
    </search>
    <add position="replace">
      <![CDATA[Opencart\Admin\Controller\Extension\Ocmod\Catalog;]]>
    </add>
  </operation>
  <operation>
    <search regex="false">
      <![CDATA[$this->load->language('catalog/attribute');]]>
    </search>
    <add position="before">
      <![CDATA[echo 'BEFORE WORKS</br>';]]>
    </add>
  </operation>
  <operation>
    <search regex="false">
      <![CDATA[$this->load->language('catalog/attribute');]]>
    </search>
    <add position="after">
      <![CDATA[echo 'AFTER WORKS</br>';]]>
    </add>
  </operation>
  <operation>
    <search regex="false">
      <![CDATA[controller_catalog_attribute]]>
    </search>
    <add position="replace">
      <![CDATA[controller_extension_ocmod_catalog_attribute]]>
    </add>
  </operation>
  <operation>
    <search regex="false">
      <![CDATA[$this->load->language('catalog/attribute');]]>
```

```
    </search>
    <add position="replace">
      <![CDATA[$this->load->language('catalog/attribute');
      echo 'REPLACE WORKS</br>';
      ]]>
    </add>
  </operation>
</file>
```

Model OCMOD code example

```
<file path="admin/model/catalog/attribute.php">
  <operation>
    <search>
      <![CDATA[Opencart\Admin\Model\Catalog;]]>
    </search>
    <add position="replace">
      <![CDATA[Opencart\Admin\Model\Extension\Ocmod\Catalog;]]>
    </add>
  </operation>
  <operation>
    <search regex="false">
      <![CDATA[public function addAttribute(array $data): int {]]>
    </search>
    <add position="before">
      <![CDATA[echo 'MODEL BEFORE WORKS</br>';]]>
    </add>
  </operation>
  <operation>
    <search regex="false">
      <![CDATA[public function addAttribute(array $data): int {]]>
    </search>
    <add position="after">
      <![CDATA[echo 'AFTER WORKS</br>';]]>
    </add>
  </operation>
</file>
```

View OCMOD example code

```
<file path="admin/view/template/catalog/attribute.twig">
  <operation>
    <search regex="false">
      <![CDATA[<div class="float-end">]]>
    </search>
    <add position="before">
      <![CDATA[       // BEFORE WORKS]]>
    </add>
  </operation>
  <operation>
```

```xml
      <search regex="false">
        <![CDATA[<div class="float-end">]]>
      </search>
      <add position="after">
        <![CDATA[     // AFTER WORKS]]>
      </add>
    </operation>
</file>
```

Library OCMOD code example

```xml
<file path="system/library/template/template.php">
    <operation>
      <search regex="false">
        <![CDATA[include]]>
      </search>
      <add position="after">
        <![CDATA[     // AFTER WORKS]]>
      </add>
    </operation>
</file>
```

Admin Extension OCMOD code example

```xml
<file path="extension/opencart/admin/controller/report/customer_order.php">
    <operation>
      <search>
        <![CDATA[Opencart\Admin\Controller\Extension\Opencart\Report;]]>
      </search>
      <add position="replace">
        <![CDATA[Opencart\Admin\Controller\Extension\Ocmod\Extension\Opencart\Report;]]>
      </add>
    </operation>
    <operation>
      <search regex="false">
        <![CDATA[$this->load->language('extension/opencart/report/customer_order');]]>
      </search>
      <add position="after">
        <![CDATA[echo 'WORKS!';]]>
      </add>
    </operation>
</file>
<file path="extension/opencart/admin/view/template/report/customer_order_form.twig">
    <operation>
      <search>
        <![CDATA[<h1>]]>
      </search>
      <add position="after">
        <![CDATA[hi]]>
      </add>
    </operation>
```

```
</operation>
</file>
```

Admin Module menu addition with OCMOD extension

We created a free module with OCMOD to show the Module link in the left menu of the admin section so that we can directly go to the Module section and don't need to keep on using the Extension filter. Here is the output.

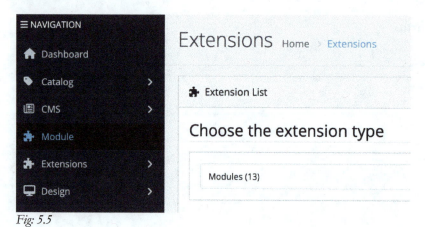

Fig: 5.5

Folder creation of OCMOD extension

- Create a folder and name it anything like for example webocreation_admin_menu
- Inside that folder create an install.json file
- Inside the webocreation_admin_menu folder, create the OCMOD folder
- Inside the OCMOD folder, create an XML file named webocreation_admin_menu.ocmod.xml

Code of install.json file

```
{
 "name": "Webocreation Admin Menu",
 "version": "1.0",
 "author": "Webocreation",
 "link": "https://www.webocreation.com"
}
```

Code of webocreation_admin_menu.ocmod.xml

```
<?xml version="1.0" encoding="utf-8"?>
<modification>
    <name>Webocreation Admin Menu</name>
    <description>Add a Module link in the top menu item in the Admin section.</description>
    <code>webocreation_admin_menu</code>
    <version>1.0</version>
    <author>Webocreation</author>
    <link>https://webocreation.com</link>
    <file path="admin/controller/common/column_left.php">
```

```
<operation>
    <search regex="false">
        <![CDATA[if ($marketplace) {]]>
    </search>
    <add position="before">
        <![CDATA[
        if ($marketplace) {
            $data['menus'][] = [
                'id'        => 'menu-extension',
                'icon'      => 'fas fa-puzzle-piece',
                'name'      => 'Module',
                'href'      => $this->url->link('marketplace/extension', 'user_token=' . $this->session-
>data['user_token'].'&type=module'),
                'children' => []
            ];
        }
        ]]>
    </add>
</operation>
</file>
</modification>
```

OCMOD error log

You can see the OCMOD error log at the Extensions >> Modifications >> Log tab. Some of the error codes:

If the search code is not found then it shows an error like the below in the Ocmod log:

MOD:
FILE: admin/controller/common/column_left.php
CODE: if ($this->user('access', 'marketplace/modification')) {
NOT FOUND - OPERATIONS ABORTED!

Read more about OCMOD

https://webocreation.com/Opencart-3-ocmod-coding-tutorial/
https://webocreation.com/ocmod-documentation/
https://www.youtube.com/watch?v=NCtiqTyEoUA
https://github.com/Opencart/Opencart/wiki/Modification-System

6. OPENCART 4 STYLES - BOOTSTRAP

OpenCart 4 leverages the power of Bootstrap 5, a popular front-end framework, to create a responsive and visually appealing e-commerce platform. Bootstrap 5 provides a robust set of CSS and JavaScript components that simplify the process of designing and developing modern web interfaces. This integration ensures that OpenCart 4 extensions and themes are mobile-friendly and consistent across different browsers and devices.

Introduction to Bootstrap in OpenCart 4

Bootstrap is an open-source toolkit for developing with HTML, CSS, and JS. It offers responsive grid systems, pre-styled components, and powerful JavaScript plugins. OpenCart 4 integrates Bootstrap to enhance the user interface (UI) and user experience (UX) of both the front end and the admin panel.

Key Benefits of Using Bootstrap in OpenCart

- **Responsive Design:** Bootstrap's grid system creates fluid and adaptive layouts that work seamlessly on desktops, tablets, and mobile devices.
- **Consistent Styling:** Predefined styles and components ensure a consistent look and feel across the site.
- **Ease of Use:** Developers can quickly implement UI components without writing extensive CSS from scratch.
- **Customizability:** Bootstrap components can be easily customized to match the specific design requirements of the store.

Bootstrap Components in OpenCart

OpenCart utilizes various Bootstrap components to build its UI. Some key components include:
- **Grid System:** Used for layout and structure, allowing for responsive designs.
- **Navigation:** Responsive navigation bars (navbars) for creating menus and headers.
- **Forms:** Pre-styled form controls for consistent and user-friendly form design.
- **Buttons:** Styled buttons with various states and sizes.
- **Modals:** Dialog boxes   and pop-ups for alerts, confirmations, and other interactions.
- **Alerts:** Feedback messages for errors, warnings, and informational content.

Integrating Bootstrap in OpenCart Themes

When developing or customizing themes in OpenCart 4, Bootstrap can be integrated and utilized to enhance the design. Here's a basic example of how to integrate Bootstrap into an OpenCart theme.

Including Bootstrap CSS

The Bootstrap CSS file needs to be included in the theme's header file. This is typically done in the header.twig template located in the theme's extension/webocreation/catalog/view/template/common/ directory.

```
<!DOCTYPE html>
<html dir="{{ direction }}" lang="{{ lang }}">
<head>
 <meta charset="UTF-8"/>
 <meta name="viewport" content="width=device-width, initial-scale=1">
 <meta http-equiv="X-UA-Compatible" content="IE=edge">
 <title>{{ title }}</title>
 <base href="{{ base }}"/>
 {% if description %}
   <meta name="description" content="{{ description }}"/>
 {% endif %}
 {% if keywords %}
   <meta name="keywords" content="{{ keywords }}"/>
 {% endif %}
 <script src="{{ jquery }}" type="text/javascript"></script>
 <link href="{{ bootstrap }}" type="text/css" rel="stylesheet" media="screen"/>
 <link href="{{ icons }}" type="text/css" rel="stylesheet"/>
 <link href="{{ stylesheet }}" type="text/css" rel="stylesheet"/>
 <script src="catalog/view/javascript/common.js" type="text/javascript"></script>
 {% for style in styles %}
   <link href="{{ style.href }}" type="text/css" rel="{{ style.rel }}" media="{{ style.media }}"/>
 {% endfor %}
 {% for script in scripts %}
   <script src="{{ script.href }}" type="text/javascript"></script>
 {% endfor %}
 {% for link in links %}
   <link href="{{ link.href }}" rel="{{ link.rel }}"/>
 {% endfor %}
 {% for analytic in analytics %}
   {{ analytic }}
 {% endfor %}
 <link href="extension/webocreation/catalog/view/stylesheet/stylesheet.css" type="text/css" rel="stylesheet"/>
</head>
<body>
<header>
 <div class="container">
   <div class="row">
```

OTHER HEADER CONTENT WILL BE HERE
* </div>*
* </div>*
</header>
<main>

Look at this line of code **< link href = "{{ bootstrap }}" type = "text/css" rel = "stylesheet"
media = "screen"/>**, the {{bootstrap}} is the link for the bootstrap css *catalog/view/stylesheet/bootstrap.css*.
With this, you can start using the Opencart bootstrap classes in your theme. While Bootstrap provides a
comprehensive set of styles out of the box, you may need to customize it to better fit your store's branding.
This can be done by overriding Bootstrap's default styles in your theme's stylesheet. Another line of code that
we added at the end of the head as an example is **<link
href="extension/webocreation/catalog/view/stylesheet/stylesheet.css" type="text/css"
rel="stylesheet"/>,** this is the webocreation theme stylesheet.css link so you can add any CSS in that
stylesheet.css and brand as per your style and needs.

Using Bootstrap Grid System

Bootstrap's grid system can be used to create responsive layouts. Below is an example of how to use the grid
system.

```
<div class="row row-cols-1 row-cols-sm-2 row-cols-md-3 row-cols-xl-4">
  <div class="col mb-3">
   Content Here
  </div>
  <div class="col mb-3">
   Content Here
  </div>
  <div class="col mb-3">
   Content Here
  </div>
  <div class="col mb-3">
   Content Here
  </div>
</div>
```

Check this *class="row row-cols-1 row-cols-sm-2 row-cols-md-3 row-cols-xl-4"*, as per the Opencart and bootstrap one
column per row will show in extra small size devices <576px, two columns per row will show in small size
devices >=576px and <768, three columns per row will show in medium size devices >=768 and <992, and
four columns per row will show >=992 devices sizes.

Creating Forms with Bootstrap

Bootstrap makes it easy to create styled and responsive forms. Here's an example of a login form using
Bootstrap components.

```
<!-- catalog/view/template/account/login.twig -->
<form id="form-login" action="{{ login }}" method="post" data-oc-toggle="ajax">
  <h2>{{ text_returning_customer }}</h2>
```

```
<p><strong>{{ text_i_am_returning_customer }}</strong></p>
<div class="mb-3">
  <label for="input-email" class="col-form-label">{{ entry_email }}</label>
  <input type="text" name="email" value="{{ email }}" placeholder="{{ entry_email }}" id="input-email"
class="form-control"/>
</div>
<div class="mb-3">
  <label for="input-password" class="col-form-label">{{ entry_password }}</label>
  <input type="password" name="password" value="{{ password }}" placeholder="{{ entry_password }}" id="input-
password" class="form-control mb-1"/>
  <a href="{{ forgotten }}">{{ text_forgotten }}</a>
</div>
{% if redirect %}
  <input type="hidden" name="redirect" value="{{ redirect }}"/>
{% endif %}
<div class="text-end">
  <button type="submit" class="btn btn-primary">{{ button_login }}</button>
</div>
</form>
```

You can see all input fields have **class = "form-control"** which is a bootstrap way to style the input field. Likewise, for buttons the class is **class = "btn btn-primary"**

Customizing Bootstrap in OpenCart

While Bootstrap provides a comprehensive set of styles out of the box, you may need to customize it to better fit your store's branding. This can be done by overriding Bootstrap's default styles in your theme's stylesheet. For example, you can create a file at extension/webocreation/catalog/view/stylesheet/stylesheet.css and add CSS as per your brand and needs

```css
body {
    font-family: 'Arial', sans-serif;
}
.btn-primary {
    background-color: #007bff;
    border-color: #007bff;
}
.product-item {
    border: 1px solid #ddd;
    padding: 10px;
    margin-bottom: 20px;
    text-align: center;
}
.product-item img {
    max-width: 100%;
    height: auto;
}
```

OpenCart 4's integration with Bootstrap significantly enhances the framework's design and usability capabilities. By utilizing Bootstrap's robust set of components and responsive grid system, developers can create modern, visually appealing, and responsive e-commerce websites. Understanding how to integrate and customize Bootstrap within OpenCart allows for a more streamlined development process and results in a better user experience for both the store owner and the customers.

JavaScript Interactions

Bootstrap 5 includes a suite of JavaScript components such as tooltips, popovers, and dropdowns, which Opencart integrates to provide interactive elements on its pages. Bootstrap JS components explicitly require our JavaScript and Popper and here are some components that you can use:

- Alerts for dismissing
- Buttons for toggling states and checkbox/radio functionality
- Carousel for all slide behaviors, controls, and indicators
- Collapse for toggling visibility of content
- Dropdowns for displaying and positioning (also requires Popper)
- Modals for displaying, positioning, and scroll behavior
- Navbar for extending our Collapse and Offcanvas plugins to implement responsive behaviors
- Navs with the Tab plugin for toggling content panes
- Off Canvases for displaying, positioning, and scroll behavior
- Scrollspy for scroll behavior and navigation updates
- Toasts for displaying and dismissing
- Tooltips and popovers for displaying and positioning (also requires Popper)

Tooltip example

```
<button type="button" class="btn btn-secondary" data-bs-toggle="tooltip" data-bs-placement="top" title="Tooltip on top">Hover me</button>
```

Popover example

```
<button type="button" class="btn btn-secondary" data-bs-toggle="popover" data-bs-content="This is a popover!">Click me</button>
```

Integrating Bootstrap in OpenCart Extensions

Extensions can be shown in left or right layout, top or bottom layout, or middle layout, because of that you need to make extensions to adjust as per the layout. Here is one simple example that we can take from the Opencart default bestseller module extension. In the bestseller module extension there is a setting called the axis, go to admin >> Extensions >> Extensions >> Select Extension type module >> Install and then Edit the bestseller module, and you will see settings like the one below. The Axis field has two options: Horizontal and Vertical.

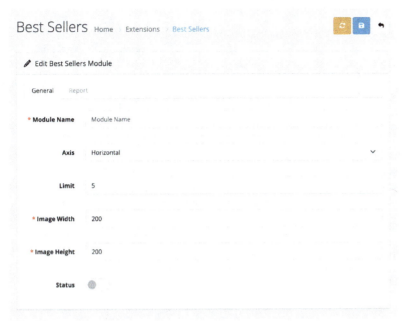

Fig: 6.1

If you want to show the module in the top, middle, or bottom layout then you will select horizontal, if you want to show it in the left or right layout then you select vertical. Here is a code example for the front end.

```
<h3>{{ heading_title }}</h3>
<div class="row{% if axis == 'horizontal' %} row-cols-1 row-cols-sm-2 row-cols-md-3 row-cols-xl-4{% endif %}">
  {% for product in products %}
    <div class="col mb-3">{{ product }}</div>
  {% endfor %}
</div>
```

As per code if you select horizontal then only these classes are added: *row-cols-1 row-cols-sm-2 row-cols-md-3 row-cols-xl-4*, with this class addition, 4 columns will show in bigger devices, 3 in medium, 2 in small, and 1 in extra small devices. In this way, you can adjust different layouts with just simply adding some classes.

Study all about bootstrap at https://getbootstrap.com/docs/5.3/getting-started/introduction, this will help you create powerful and feature-packed themes and extensions.

7. OPENCART 4 EXTENSION DEVELOPMENT

An Opencart extension previously called a module, is a self-contained piece of code that adds specific functionality or features to an Opencart store. Extensions can be used to enhance the core capabilities of Opencart by introducing new elements such as payment gateways, shipping methods, product displays, customer interactions, analytics, product feeds, and much more. They are designed to be easily installed, configured, and managed within the Opencart administrative interface. Now in Opencart 4, theme is also taken as extension.

Key Features of Opencart Extensions

As a developer you should always think about following key features of Opencart extensions while developing them.

MVCL folder structure:

All extensions follow the MVCL folder structure.

Everything multi: language, store, layout, and currency

All extensions should support multilingual, multi-currency, multi-layout, and multi-currency.

Ease of Installation:

Extension can be installed quickly through the Opencart admin panel. Most extensions are available as downloadable packages that can be uploaded and installed directly from the admin interface.

Configurability:

Once installed, extensions typically provide a set of configuration options that can be adjusted to meet the specific needs of your store. The settings for each module are usually accessible through the admin panel, under the Extensions section.

Modularity:

Extensions are designed to work independently of each other, allowing you to add, remove, or update them without affecting the rest of your store. This modularity ensures that you can customize your store's functionality incrementally and flexibly.

Wide Range of Functions:

Extensions cover a vast array of functionalities, from enhancing SEO to integrating third-party services like payment gateways, feeds, shipping, analytics, social media platforms, etc. Common types of extensions include analytics, captchas, Currency rates, dashboards, feeds, anti-fraud, languages, marketplaces, modules, payments, reports, shipping, themes, and order totals

Community and Third-Party Development:

Opencart's large community and marketplace offer numerous free and paid modules developed by third-party developers. These modules can significantly extend the functionality of your store beyond the default capabilities of Opencart.

Types of Opencart Extensions

Opencart extensions are categorized into different types as per their functionalities. You can see them at Admin >> Extensions >> Extensions and see the different types in the dropdown.

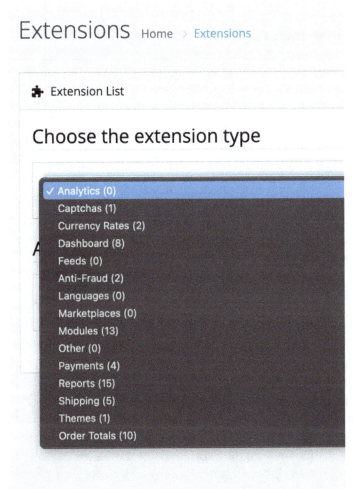

Fig: 7.1

Analytics:

In Analytics Opencart extensions, include extensions related to the analytics, for example, Google Analytics which you can use for tracking and analytics.

Captchas:

In Captchas Opencart extensions you can include extensions related to the captchas, like basic captcha, google recaptcha v2, and v3, Hcaptcha, etc.

Currency rates:

In Currency rate extensions you can include third-party currency rate exchange extension which is used to update the price as per the currency selected.

Other extensions:

Dashboard extensions are shown on the administrative main page where each widget is one dashboard extension. **Feeds** extensions are for sitemaps, feeds, etc, and can be used to create Google sitemaps, google merchant feeds, Openbay pro feed, etc. **Anti-fraud** extensions are fraud-related and can be used for FraudLabs Pro, Anti-Fraud IP, and MaxMind Anti-Fraud. **Language** extensions are for different languages. Similar to other types of marketplaces, modules, payments, reports, shipping, themes, and order total.

Difference between Single Instance module and Multi-instance module

We are showing you the difference between the coding structure of a single instance Opencart module and Opencart multi-instance module both in the admin section and the catalog section.

Single Instance Opencart module	Multi-Instance Opencart module
After installation, it will create only one module	After installation, it can create many modules as needed
 Fig: 7.2	
Examples of core available only one instance Opencart module are: Account module, Category module, Information module, etc	Examples of core available multi-instance Opencart modules are the Banner module, Bestsellers module, Carousel module, Featured module, latest module, slideshow module, special module, etc.
Admin section code change	
$this->load->model('setting/setting');	*$this->load->model('setting/module');*
$this->model_setting_setting->editSetting('module_login', $this->request->post);	*if (!isset($this->request->get['module_id'])) {* *$this->model_setting_module->addModule('bestseller', $this->request->post);* *} else {* *$this->model_setting_module->editModule($this->request->get['module_id'], $this->request->post);*

	}
The name of the form field should start with the extension initials, for the module, it is like name="module_*****", for the shipping extension, it is like name="shipping_***", for the payment extension name="payment_***" etc.	The name of the form field can be any
Data are saved in the oc_setting database table	Data are saved in the oc_module database table
Catalog section code change	
The code difference in the controller is at the index method. public function index() {	public function index($setting) {
In the oc_layout database table, the cod will be stored in the code column	In the oc_layout database table, the code dot module ID is stored in the code column

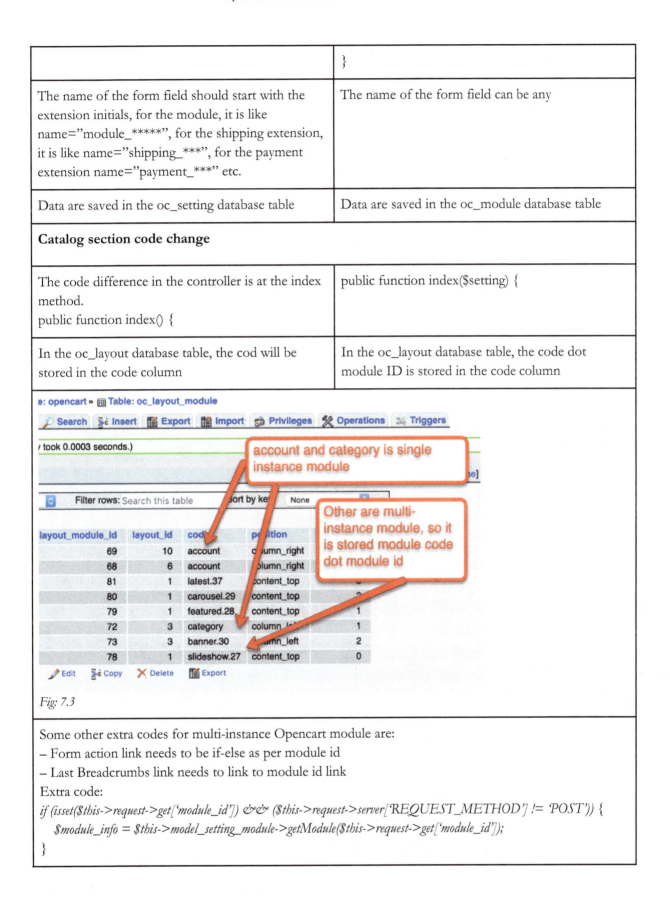

Fig: 7.3

Some other extra codes for multi-instance Opencart module are:

– Form action link needs to be if-else as per module id

– Last Breadcrumbs link needs to link to module id link

Extra code:

if (isset($this->request->get['module_id']) && ($this->request->server['REQUEST_METHOD'] != 'POST')) {

$module_info = $this->model_setting_module->getModule($this->request->get['module_id']);

}

Create custom Analytics extension in Opencart 4

With the launch of Opencart 4 you will not find the Google Analytics Opencart 4 module that we used to have in Opencart 3, so to fulfill that requirement let's create a custom analytics Opencart 4 extension called Third Party JS extension where you can add the Javascript code provided by third-party like Google Analytics, Facebook pixel, etc and add it on this extension. https://github.com/rupaknepali/Opencart-free-modules/raw/master/Third-Party-JS-Opencart-4/third_party_js.ocmod.zip

How to install the Opencart 4 extension?

Log in to Admin >> Extensions >> Installer >> Click the Upload button and select the file that ends with .ocmod.zip. In the above download example, it is **thirdpartyjs.ocmod.zip**. Once it is installed you will see the "Third Party JS" in the installed extensions.

Once you upload the zip file, you click the install green icon to install the extension.

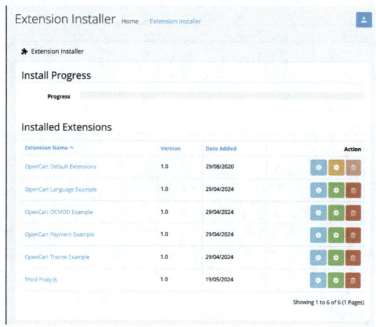

Fig: 7.4

Once you click the install button, your extension is installed successfully. Once you see the success message. Now you can go to Admin >> Extensions >> Extension. Then, choose the extension type "Analytics" and click the install green install button.

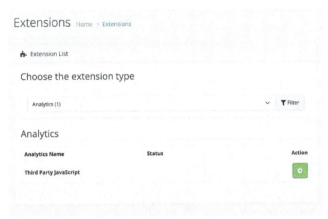

Fig: 7.5

Once you click the install button, you can edit the store and you will see a form where you can install the third-party JavaScript like below, enable the status, and click the blue save button.

Fig: 7.6

After clicking the save, now the JavaScript code is shown at the head tag.

```
<head>
  <meta charset="UTF-8"/>
  <meta name="viewport" content="width=device-width, initial-scale=1"/>
  <meta http-equiv="X-UA-Compatible" content="IE=edge">
  <title>Your Store</title>
  <base href="http://opencart.loc/"/>
    <meta name="description" content="My Store"/>
    <script src="catalog/view/javascript/jquery/jquery-3.7.1.min.js" type="text/javascript"></script>
  <link href="catalog/view/stylesheet/bootstrap.css" type="text/css" rel="stylesheet" media="screen"/>
  <link href="catalog/view/stylesheet/fonts/fontawesome/css/all.min.css" type="text/css" rel="stylesheet"/>
  <link href="catalog/view/stylesheet/stylesheet.css" type="text/css" rel="stylesheet"/>
  <script src="catalog/view/javascript/common.js" type="text/javascript"></script>
    <!-- Google tag (gtag.js) -->
<script async src="https://www.googletagmanager.com/gtag/js?id=G-JGEXGRV8XF"></script>
<script>
  window.dataLayer = window.dataLayer || [];
  function gtag(){dataLayer.push(arguments);}
  gtag('js', new Date());

  gtag('config', 'G-JGEXGRV8XF');
</script>
  </head>
```

Fig: 7.7

In this way, you can install the Opencart 4 extensions and use a custom Opencart 4 analytics extension.

Files and folder structure of the Opencart 4 extension

In Opencart 4, the extension folder is available in the root folder. When you see in the extension folder, by default there is an opencart folder, ocmod/ folder, and index.html. In the opencart folder, you will see all default extensions provided by Opencart. Here we already installed the thirdpartyjs analytics extension because of which you are seeing the thirdpartyjs/ folder, its subfolders, and file.

Fig: 7.8

Naming tips for custom Opencart 4 extensions

- The file name should be between 1 letter and up to 128 letters.
- The filename should end with ".ocmod.zip"
- The uploaded file should not exceed the max file size: of 32 megabytes
- The Opencart extension installer checks if the file already exists, if it exists then it will throw an error.
- It validates if the file can be opened and if there is an install.json that can be read. So, every extension should have install.json
- All form fields should start with extension type and then the extension name
- Admin namespace can be named as
  namespace Opencart\Admin\Controller\Extension\ExtensionFolderName\ExtensionType;
  Catalog namespace can be named as
  namespace Opencart\Catalog\Controller\Extension\ExtensionFolderName\ExtensionType;
- Class name should be same as file name without php extension

Create an install.json file in the Opencart extension

Create a folder, in our example, it is "thirdpartyjs" and inside it create a file name called install.json. It supports the following keys: name, version, author, and link. As per our extension, the following is an example:

```
{
 "name": "Third Praty Js",
 "description": "This extension is used for adding Third party Js like Google Analytics, Facebook Pixels, etc",
 "version": "1.0",
 "author": "Webocreation",
 "link": "https://webocreation.com"
}
```

Once install.json is inside the folder, you can zip it and name it that ends with .ocmod.zip, then upload it from the Opencart extension installer. For our example, we named it thirdpartyjs.ocmod.zip and uploaded it to Admin >> Extensions >> Installer and clicked the upload blue button and you will see it like in the image above 7.4. While uploading, if you don't get anything then you need to go to the storage folder, and inside it see the marketplace folder and remove the existing zip file. With this, you are ready to start coding and adding files for your extension. Now, we create an admin section for the Third Party Js extension.

Admin Section for ThirdPartyJs analytics extension

Admin Controller

```php
<?php
namespace Opencart\Admin\Controller\Extension\Thirdpartyjs\Analytics;
/**
* Class Thirdpartyjs
*
* @package Opencart\Admin\Controller\Extension\Thirdpartyjs\Analytics
*/
class Thirdpartyjs extends \Opencart\System\Engine\Controller {
  /**
  * Index
  *
  * @return void
  */
  public function index(): void {
    $this->load->language('extension/thirdpartyjs/analytics/thirdpartyjs');
    $this->document->setTitle($this->language->get('heading_title'));
    $data['breadcrumbs'] = [];
    $data['breadcrumbs'][] = [
      'text' => $this->language->get('text_home'),
      'href' => $this->url->link('common/dashboard', 'user_token=' . $this->session->data['user_token'])
    ];
    $data['breadcrumbs'][] = [
      'text' => $this->language->get('text_extension'),
      'href' => $this->url->link('marketplace/extension', 'user_token=' . $this->session->data['user_token'] .
'&type=analytics)
    ];
    $data['breadcrumbs'][] = [
      'text' => $this->language->get('heading_title'),
      'href' => $this->url->link('extension/thirdpartyjs/analytics/thirdpartyjs', 'user_token=' . $this->session-
>data['user_token'])
    ];
    $data['save'] = $this->url->link('extension/thirdpartyjs/analytics/thirdpartyjs.save', 'user_token=' . $this->session-
>data['user_token']);
    $data['back'] = $this->url->link('marketplace/extension', 'user_token=' . $this->session->data['user_token'] .
'&type=analytics);
    $data['analytics_thirdpartyjs_status'] = $this->config->get('analytics_thirdpartyjs_status');
    $data['analytics_thirdpartyjs_code'] = $this->config->get('analytics_thirdpartyjs_code');
    $data['header'] = $this->load->controller('common/header');
    $data['column_left'] = $this->load->controller('common/column_left');
    $data['footer'] = $this->load->controller('common/footer');
    $this->response->setOutput($this->load->view('extension/thirdpartyjs/analytics/thirdpartyjs', $data));
}
/**
* Save
*
* @return void
*/
public function save(): void {
```

69

```
$this->load->language('extension/thirdpartyjs/analytics/thirdpartyjs');
$json = [];
if (!$this->user->hasPermission('modify', 'extension/thirdpartyjs/analytics/thirdpartyjs')) {
  $json['error'] = $this->language->get('error_permission');
}
if (!$json) {
  $this->load->model('setting/setting');
  $this->model_setting_setting->editSetting('analytics_thirdpartyjs', $this->request->post);
  $json['success'] = $this->language->get('text_success');
}
$this->response->addHeader('Content-Type: application/json');
$this->response->setOutput(json_encode($json));
  }
}
```

Here are some explanation of some code:
As mentioned the Admin namespace can be named as
namespace Opencart\Admin\Controller\Extension**ExtensionFolderName\ExtensionType**;
Here extension folder name is thirdpartyjs and the extension type is analytics so the namespace becomes:
namespace Opencart\Admin\Controller\Extension\Thirdpartyjs\Analytics;

The filename is thirdpartyjs.php so the class name is Thirdpartyjs, it should always extend the
\Opencart\System\Engine\Controller.

class Thirdpartyjs extends \Opencart\System\Engine\Controller {

In this example we have two methods index() and save(), you can have any methods as per your business requirements or logic. In most of the extensions, they need to have a setting page for configuration so index() is to load everything, and save() is to save the form data. In some advanced extensions you may need to create your database table while installing then you can use the install() method which is called automatically when a module is installed. Likewise, there is an uninstall() method which is also called automatically when a module is uninstalled. You can look into the Opencart default extension
/extension/opencart/admin/controller/fraud/ip.php where you can see how the install and uninstall methods are set up calling the model and querying the database table.

```
/**
 * Install
 *
 * @return void
 */
public function install(): void {
    if ($this->user->hasPermission('modify', 'extension/fraud')) {
        $this->load->model('extension/opencart/fraud/ip');
        $this->model_extension_opencart_fraud_ip->install();
    }
}
/**
 * Uninstall
 *
 * @return void
 */
```

```
public function uninstall(): void {
    if ($this->user->hasPermission('modify', 'extension/fraud')) {
        $this->load->model('extension/opencart/fraud/ip');
        $this->model_extension_opencart_fraud_ip->uninstall();
    }
}
```

Index method:

We write this line of code to load the language file created at *thirdpartyjs/admin/language/en-gb/analytics/thirdpartyjs.php*

$this->load->language('extension/thirdpartyjs/analytics/thirdpartyjs');

Opencart uses *.METHODNAME* to call the method. Here .save is calling the save method. In some old 4 versions |*save* was used, now dot method name is used.

$data['save'] = $this->url->link('extension/thirdpartyjs/analytics/thirdpartyjs.save', 'user_token=' . $this->session->data['user_token']);

All form field names should start with extension type and the extension name and field unique name and assign the value like this so if the value is already set it is assigned to the field.

$data['analytics_thirdpartyjs_status'] = $this->config->get('analytics_thirdpartyjs_status');
$data['analytics_thirdpartyjs_code'] = $this->config->get('analytics_thirdpartyjs_code');

All field values are saved in oc_setting database table oc_ is the database prefix here. By doing $this->config->get, you are getting the value of the mentioned key from the oc_setting database table.

▼ setting_id	store_id	code	key	value	serialized
226	0	analytics_thirdpartyjs	analytics_thirdpartyjs_code	<!-- Google tag (gtag.js) --> <script as...	0
227	0	analytics_thirdpartyjs	analytics_thirdpartyjs_status	1	0

Fig: 7.9

You can pass a controller in the data variable that loads in the view, here $data['header'] is assigned with a common header controller, and the header controller is loaded in the view by {{header}}, same for other data variables.
$data['header'] = $this->load->controller('common/header');
$data['column_left'] = $this->load->controller('common/column_left');
$data['footer'] = $this->load->controller('common/footer');

Save method

In the save method, all other code is self-explanatory, below two lines are the one which saves all form POST data to the setting database table. You should always pass the extension type and the extension name. Here you are passing 'analytics_thirdpartyjs' where analytics is the extension type and thirdpartyjs is the extension name.
$this->load->model('setting/setting');
$this->model_setting_setting->editSetting('analytics_thirdpartyjs', $this->request->post);

Here is the details in the image of the code:

Fig: 7.10

If you are creating a payment extension then in the edit setting you need to pass payment_extensionname, if shipping extension you pass shipping_extensionname, same for other, here is the table

Extension type	Value to pass
Analytics	analytics_
Captcha	captcha_
Currency	currency_
Dashboard	dashboard_
Feed	feed_
Fraud	fraud_

Extension type	Value to pass
Module	module_
Payment	payment_
Report	report_
Shipping	shipping_
Theme	theme_
Total	total_

Admin Language

This language file is used to manage and support multiple languages for the store's front end and admin interface. This file contains all the textual content displayed to the user, allowing for easy translation and localization. Each language has its own set of files that map specific language keys to their respective translations.

```php
<?php
// Heading
$_['heading_title']    = 'Third Party Javascript';
// Text
$_['text_extension']   = 'Extensions';
$_['text_success']     = 'Success: You have modified Third Party Js!';
$_['text_edit']        = 'Edit Third Party Js';
// Entry
$_['entry_js_script']  = 'Enter Javascript code';
$_['entry_script_code'] = '<script>....</script>';
$_['entry_status']     = 'Status';
// Error
$_['error_permission'] = 'Warning: You do not have permission to modify Third Party Js!';
```

Admin View

This view file defines the HTML structure and layout of the admin interface, which utilizes the Twig templating engine, which allows for cleaner and more readable templates by separating PHP logic from HTML content.

```
{{ header }}{{ column_left }}
<div id="content">
  <div class="page-header">
    <div class="container-fluid">
      <div class="float-end">
        <button type="submit" form="form-thirdpartyjs" data-bs-toggle="tooltip" title="{{ button_save }}" class="btn btn-primary"><i class="fa-solid fa-save"></i></button>
        <a href="{{ back }}" data-bs-toggle="tooltip" title="{{ button_back }}" class="btn btn-light"><i class="fa-solid fa-reply"></i></a></div>
```

```
<h1>{{ heading_title }}</h1>
<ol class="breadcrumb">
  {% for breadcrumb in breadcrumbs %}
    <li class="breadcrumb-item"><a href="{{ breadcrumb.href }}">{{ breadcrumb.text }}</a></li>
  {% endfor %}
</ol>
</div>
</div>
<div class="container-fluid">
  <div class="card">
    <div class="card-header"><i class="fa-solid fa-pencil"></i> {{ text_edit }}</div>
    <div class="card-body">
      <form id="form-captcha" action="{{ save }}" method="post" data-oc-toggle="ajax">
        <div class="row mb-3">
          <label class="col-sm-2 col-form-label">{{ entry_js_script}}</label>
          <div class="col-sm-10">
            <textarea name="analytics_thirdpartyjs_code" rows="5" placeholder="{{ entry_script_code }}" id="input-code"
class="form-control">{{ analytics_thirdpartyjs_code }}</textarea>
            {% if error_code %}
            <div class="text-danger">{{ error_code }}</div>
            {% endif %}
          </div>
        </div>
        <div class="row mb-3">
          <label class="col-sm-2 col-form-label">{{ entry_status }}</label>
          <div class="col-sm-10">
            <div class="form-check form-switch form-switch-lg">
              <input type="hidden" name="analytics_thirdpartyjs_status" value="0"/>
              <input type="checkbox" name="analytics_thirdpartyjs_status" value="1" id="input-status" class="form-check-
input"{% if analytics_thirdpartyjs_status %} checked{% endif %}/>
            </div>
          </div>
        </div>
      </form>
    </div>
  </div>
</div>
{{ footer }}
```

All twig variables are defined either in the controller or in the language like {{header}}, {{footer}} etc are defined in the controller, {{button_save}} are in the language file. We are explaining some of the code above. The first one is of the Save button code:

```
<button type="submit" form="form-captcha" data-bs-toggle="tooltip" title="{{ button_save }}" class="btn btn-
primary"><i class="fa-solid fa-save"></i></button>
```

This button form name and the form id need to be the same. Here in the above example the button attribute *form="form-captcha"* is the same name as the form's id

<form id="form-captcha" action="{{ save }}" method="post" data-oc-toggle="ajax">

All form fields should start with extension type and then the extension name. Here all fields start with analytics_thirdparty. The extension type is analytics and the extension name we created is third party. See the power of *data-oc-toggle="ajax" All* saving functionalities happen with ajax, so if ajax is not happening then look into if you have added these attributes in the form.

To get the On/Off design instead of the select box, you need to use like below code in Opencart:

<div class="form-check form-switch form-switch-lg">

  <input type="hidden" name="analytics_thirdpartyjs_status" value="0"/>

  <input type="checkbox" name="analytics_thirdpartyjs_status" value="1" id="input-status" class="form-check-input"{% if analytics_thirdpartyjs_status %} checked{% endif %}/>

</div>

Others are self-explanatory

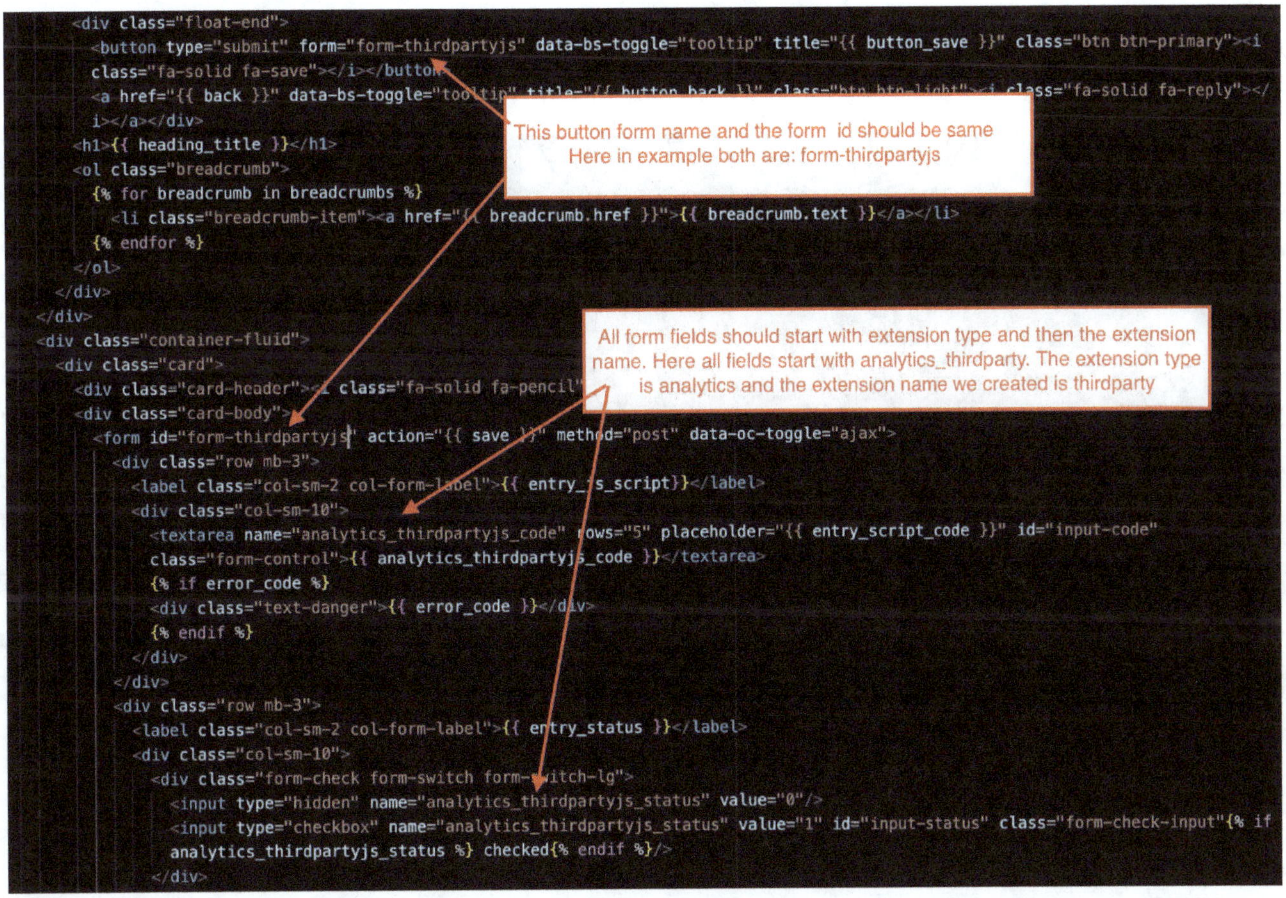

```
<div class="float-end">
  <button type="submit" form="form-thirdpartyjs" data-bs-toggle="tooltip" title="{{ button_save }}" class="btn btn-primary"><i
  class="fa-solid fa-save"></i></button>
  <a href="{{ back }}" data-bs-toggle="tooltip" title="{{ button_back }}" class="btn btn-light"><i class="fa-solid fa-reply"></
  i></a></div>
<h1>{{ heading_title }}</h1>
<ol class="breadcrumb">
  {% for breadcrumb in breadcrumbs %}
    <li class="breadcrumb-item"><a href="{{ breadcrumb.href }}">{{ breadcrumb.text }}</a></li>
  {% endfor %}
</ol>
</div>
</div>
<div class="container-fluid">
<div class="card">
  <div class="card-header"><i class="fa-solid fa-pencil"
  <div class="card-body">
    <form id="form-thirdpartyjs" action="{{ save }}" method="post" data-oc-toggle="ajax">
      <div class="row mb-3">
        <label class="col-sm-2 col-form-label">{{ entry_js_script}}</label>
        <div class="col-sm-10">
          <textarea name="analytics_thirdpartyjs_code" rows="5" placeholder="{{ entry_script_code }}" id="input-code"
          class="form-control">{{ analytics_thirdpartyjs_code }}</textarea>
          {% if error_code %}
          <div class="text-danger">{{ error_code }}</div>
          {% endif %}
        </div>
      </div>
      <div class="row mb-3">
        <label class="col-sm-2 col-form-label">{{ entry_status }}</label>
        <div class="col-sm-10">
          <div class="form-check form-switch form-switch-lg">
            <input type="hidden" name="analytics_thirdpartyjs_status" value="0"/>
            <input type="checkbox" name="analytics_thirdpartyjs_status" value="1" id="input-status" class="form-check-input"{% if
            analytics_thirdpartyjs_status %} checked{% endif %}/>
          </div>
```

> This button form name and the form id should be same
> Here in example both are: form-thirdpartyjs

> All form fields should start with extension type and then the extension name. Here all fields start with analytics_thirdparty. The extension type is analytics and the extension name we created is thirdparty

Fig: 7.11

Frontend Section for ThirdPartyJs analytics extension

<?php

namespace Opencart\Catalog\Controller\Extension\Thirdpartyjs\Analytics;

*/***

 ** Class Thirdpartyjs*

```
 *
 * @package Opencart\Catalog\Controller\Extension\Thirdpartyjs\Analytics
 */
class Thirdpartyjs extends \Opencart\System\Engine\Controller {
    /**
     * Index
     *
     * @return string
     */
    public function index(): string {
        return html_entity_decode($this->config->get('analytics_thirdpartyjs_code'), ENT_QUOTES, 'UTF-8');
    }
}
```

For all analytics extensions the opencart header *catalog/controller/common/header.php* get all the analytics extensions and show the code in the header by calling the active analytics extensions. The Thirdpartyjs analytics extension simply gets the 'analytics_thirdpartyjs_code' script and returns the script code by decoding.

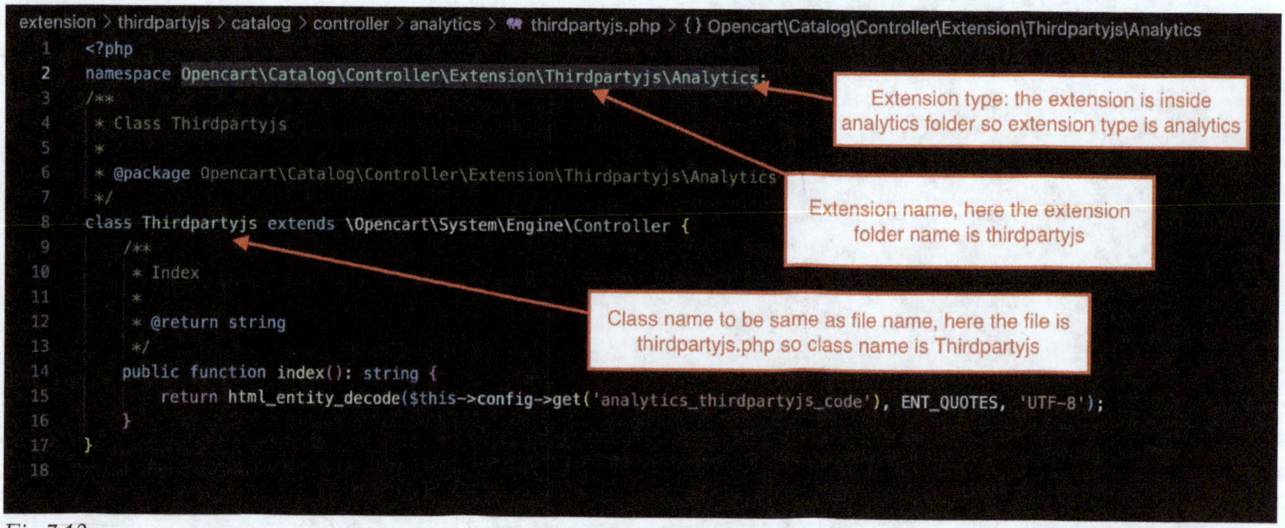

Fig: 7.12

If you are curious which code is calling all the analytics extensions then go to *catalog/controller/common/header.php* and look for the following code.

```
// Analytics
$data['analytics'] = [];
if (!$this->config->get('config_cookie_id') || (isset($this->request->cookie['policy']) && $this->request->cookie['policy'])) {
    $this->load->model('setting/extension');
    $analytics = $this->model_setting_extension->getExtensionsByType('analytics');
    foreach ($analytics as $analytic) {
        if ($this->config->get('analytics_' . $analytic['code'] . '_status')) {
            $data['analytics'][] = $this->load->controller('extension/' . $analytic['extension'] . '/analytics/' . $analytic['code'],
$this->config->get('analytics_' . $analytic['code'] . '_status'));
```

```
        }
    }
}
```

This code gets all the analytics extension *$this->model_setting_extension->getExtensionsByType('analytics');* and then the controller is called of the analytics extension by this line from the view: *$this->load->controller('extension/' . $analytic['extension'] . '/analytics/' . $analytic['code'], $this->config->get('analytics_' . $analytic['code'] . '_status'));*

If you want to have an OCMOD file inside the extension then all ****.ocmod.xml should be inside the **ocmod/** folder which we already described in Chapter 5.

8. OPENCART 4 THEME DEVELOPMENT

With the launch of Opencart 4, themes are also taken as extensions. In this chapter, we show how to install the Opencart theme and create the custom Opencart 4 theme admin section and the frontend section. You can download the theme from our GitHub as well: <u>Download the custom Opencart 4 theme</u> <u>https://github.com/rupaknepali/Opencart-free-modules/raw/master/WeboCreation-Opencart-4-custom-theme/webocreation4.ocmod.zip</u>

Install the Opencart 4 theme

Let's take an example from the downloaded zip file from the GitHub <u>link</u>. Once you download, you will get a zip file named webocreation.ocmod.zip, then go to Opencart admin >> Extensions >> Installer >> Click the blue upload button. Once the upload is completed, it will list in the Installed Extensions, when you can click the install green button.

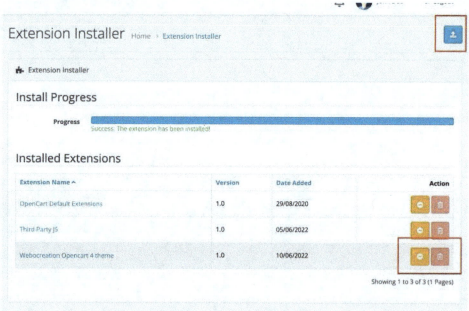

Fig: 8.1

Activate Opencart 4 theme

Now, go to Extensions >> Extensions >> Choose the extension type >> Themes

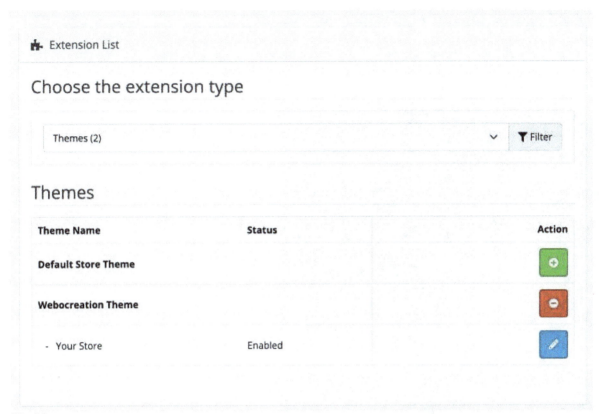

Fig: 8.2

Click the green install button on the new theme, and you can uninstall the old one. Then, click the blue edit button, change the status to enable, and click Save.

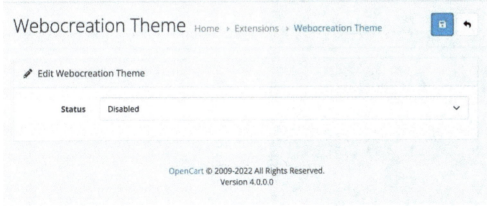

Fig: 8.3

With these, your new Opencart 4 theme is active.

Uninstall the Opencart 4 theme

Login into Opencart admin, then Extensions >> Installer >> Find the theme and click Uninstall. If you totally want to remove it then you can delete it.

Files and folders structure of the Opencart 4 theme

After installation, all theme files and folders also reside in the extension folder. Here is one example of how the admin files and folders reside, overall our main theme folder is named "webocreation" and all the controllers and language files are named as webocreation.***. You can name them as you like.

Fig: 8.4

Admin Language of custom Opencart 4 theme

Let's start by creating the language file for the Opencart 4 theme. Create files and folders like extension >> webocreation >> admin >> language >> en-gb >> theme >> webocreation.php. Here is one simple example of texts added for our custom theme.

```php
<?php
// Heading
$_['heading_title'] = 'Webocreation Theme';
// Text
$_['text_extension'] = 'Extensions';
$_['text_success'] = 'Success: You have modified the Webocreation theme!';
$_['text_edit'] = 'Edit Webocreation Theme';
// Entry
$_['entry_status'] = 'Status';
// Error
$_['error_permission'] = 'Warning: You do not have permission to modify the Webocreation theme!';
```

Admin View of custom Opencart 4 theme

Create a new file at extension >> webocreation >> admin >> view >> template >> theme and create webocreation.twig. Paste the following code. Most of the code is similar to other modules.

"CHECK THE SELECT FIELD NAME, WHICH IS NAME="theme_webocreation_status" THE NAME OF ALL THEME SETTINGS SHOULD START WITH THEME_ AND THEN WITH THE FILE NAME, AS OUR FILE NAME IS WEBOCREATION.PHP SO EACH FIELD NAME SHOULD START WITH theme_webocreation_

```twig
{{ header }}{{ column_left }}
<div id="content">
  <div class="page-header">
    <div class="container-fluid">
      <div class="float-end">
        <button type="submit" form="form-theme" data-bs-toggle="tooltip" title="{{ button_save }}" class="btn btn-primary"><i class="fas fa-save"></i></button>
        <a href="{{ back }}" data-bs-toggle="tooltip" title="{{ button_back }}" class="btn btn-light"><i class="fas fa-reply"></i></a>
      </div>
      <h1>{{ heading_title }}</h1>
      <ol class="breadcrumb">
  {% for breadcrumb in breadcrumbs %}
    <li class="breadcrumb-item"><a href="{{ breadcrumb.href }}">{{ breadcrumb.text }}</a></li>
  {% endfor %}
      </ol>
    </div>
  </div>
  <div class="container-fluid">
    <div class="card">
      <div class="card-header"><i class="fas fa-pencil-alt"></i> {{ text_edit }}</div>
      <div class="card-body">
        <form id="form-theme" action="{{ save }}" method="post" data-oc-toggle="ajax">
          <div class="row mb-3">
            <label for="input-status" class="col-sm-2 col-form-label">{{ entry_status }}</label>
            <div class="col-sm-10">
```

```
        <div class="form-check form-switch form-switch-lg">
            <input type="checkbox" name="theme_webocreation_status" value="1" id="input-status" class="form-check-
input"{% if theme_webocreation_status %} checked{% endif %} />
        </div>
      </div>
    </div>
  </form>
    </div>
  </div>
</div>
</div>
{{ footer }}
```

Only we need to make sure that the field names start with theme_webocreation_, others are similar to other modules or theme codes.

Admin Controller of custom Opencart 4 theme

Now, let's create a controller file and folders like extension >> webocreation >> admin >> controller >> theme >> webocreation.php. Now you can add the following code, we are describing some important code below:

```php
<?php
namespace Opencart\Admin\Controller\Extension\Webocreation\Theme;
class Webocreation extends \Opencart\System\Engine\Controller
{
    public function index(): void
    {
        $this->load->language('extension/webocreation/theme/webocreation');
        $this->document->setTitle($this->language->get('heading_title'));
        $data['breadcrumbs'] = [];
        $data['breadcrumbs'][] = [
            'text' => $this->language->get('text_home'),
            'href' => $this->url->link('common/dashboard', 'user_token=' . $this->session->data['user_token']),
        ];
        $data['breadcrumbs'][] = [
            'text' => $this->language->get('text_extension'),
            'href' => $this->url->link('marketplace/extension', 'user_token=' . $this->session->data['user_token'] .
'&type=theme'),
        ];
        $data['breadcrumbs'][] = [
            'text' => $this->language->get('heading_title'),
            'href' => $this->url->link('extension/webocreation/theme/webocreation', 'user_token=' . $this->session-
>data['user_token'] . '&store_id=' . $this->request->get['store_id']),
        ];
        $data['save'] = $this->url->link('extension/webocreation/theme/webocreation|save', 'user_token=' . $this->session-
```

```php
>data['user_token'] . '&store_id=' . $this->request->get['store_id']);
    $data['back'] = $this->url->link('marketplace/extension', 'user_token=' . $this->session->data['user_token'] .
'&type=theme');
    if (isset($this->request->get['store_id'])) {
        $this->load->model('setting/setting');
        $setting_info = $this->model_setting_setting->getSetting('theme_webocreation', $this->request->get['store_id']);
    }
    if (isset($setting_info['theme_webocreation_status'])) {
        $data['theme_webocreation_status'] = $setting_info['theme_webocreation_status'];
    } else {
        $data['theme_webocreation_status'] = '';
    }
    $data['header'] = $this->load->controller('common/header');
    $data['column_left'] = $this->load->controller('common/column_left');
    $data['footer'] = $this->load->controller('common/footer');
    $this->response->setOutput($this->load->view('extension/webocreation/theme/webocreation, $data));
}
public function save(): void
{
    $this->load->language('extension/webocreation/theme/webocreation');
    $json = [];
    if (!$this->user->hasPermission('modify', 'extension/webocreation/theme/webocreation')) {
        $json['error'] = $this->language->get('error_permission');
    }
    if (!$json) {
        $this->load->model('setting/setting');
        $this->model_setting_setting->editSetting('theme_webocreation_status', $this->request->post, $this->request-
>get['store_id']);
        $json['success'] = $this->language->get('text_success');
    }
    $this->response->addHeader('Content-Type: application/json');
    $this->response->setOutput(json_encode($json));
}
public function install(): void
{
    if ($this->user->hasPermission('modify', 'extension/webocreation/theme/webocreation)) {
        $this->load->model('setting/startup');
        $this->model_setting_startup->addStartup('theme_webocreation',
'catalog/extension/webocreation/startup/webocreation', 1, 2);
    }
}
public function uninstall(): void
{
    if ($this->user->hasPermission('modify', 'extension/webocreation/theme/webocreation)) {
        $this->load->model('setting/startup');
```

```
        $this->model_setting_startup->deleteStartupByCode('theme_webocreation');
    }
  }
}
```

Opencart 4 started using namespace, a powerful concept that provides a way to organize code into groups that allow you to create reusable components that can be reused across multiple projects. So, each Opencart module, theme, and all extensions now start with a namespace. As we are creating a theme at the end it is Theme, if you are creating a module, it will be Module, if you are creating an analytics extension then it will be Analytics.

namespace Opencart\Admin\Controller\Extension\Webocreation\Theme;

In the second line, we create the class with the name same as the file, as our file name is standard.php, so we name the class as Standard and inherit the main Opencart controller.

class Webocreation extends \Opencart\System\Engine\Controller

Now, we create an index method and add the return type

public function index(): void

In the index method, all other codes are similar to other modules and extensions, one line of code that you need to look at is below where you add the webocreation as the first parameter. This first parameter and each field name of the form should start with the same so here in our example is webocreation

$setting_info = $this->model_setting_setting->getSetting('webocreation', $this->request->get['store_id']);

Another code to look into is below, right now we have one field so it is like below, you need to do something similar for each field that you will add. $setting_info holds all the settings that are given by the above getSetting method.

if (isset($setting_info['webocreation_status'])) {
  $data['webocreation_status'] = $setting_info['webocreation_status'];
} else {
  $data['webocreation_status'] = '';
}

Another is the save method:

public function save(): void

In the same method, look into one main line of code which is like below:

$this->model_setting_setting->editSetting('webocreation', $this->request->post, $this->request->get['store_id']);

The first parameter of the editSetting method should be webocreation. Above is the main code that we need to check and change, similar to all other Opencart 4 modules or extensions or themes.

public function install(): void {
  if ($this->user->hasPermission('modify', 'extension/webocreation/theme/standard')) {
    $this->load->model('setting/startup');

```
    $this->model_setting_startup->addStartup('webocreation', 'catalog/extension/webocreation/startup/standard', 1, 2);
  }
}
```

The above code will add the Startup like below which we will be using in the catalog code, which we will show in the next upcoming post.

Opencart Startup Theme

Likewise, we add the uninstall code like the one below so that all rows are removed from the database

```
public function uninstall(): void {
  if ($this->user->hasPermission('modify', 'extension/webocreation/theme/standard')) {
    $this->load->model('setting/startup');
    $this->model_setting_startup->deleteStartupByCode('webocreation');
  }
}
```

As part of the Opencart 4 theme development tutorial, We already showed you how to install the Opencart 4 theme and to create the Opencart 4 custom theme admin section, in today's tutorial, we are showing you how to develop the frontend section of the Opencart 4 custom theme. OC 4 doesn't use the default folder name, by default. It uses the extension folder from the beginning.

When we developed the backend code, we added the Startup code like the below

Fig: 8.5

Frontend Controller of the custom Opencart 4 theme

Taking Startup UI into consideration, you need to create the following file at extension >> webocreation >> catalog >> controller >> startup >> webocreation.php, once you create the file, you can use the following lines of code.

```
<?php
namespace Opencart\Catalog\Controller\Extension\webocreation\Startup;
class Webocreation extends \Opencart\System\Engine\Controller
```

85

```
{
    public function index(): void
    {
        if ($this->config->get('theme_webocreation_status')) {
            $this->event->register('view/*/before', new
\Opencart\System\Engine\Action('extension/webocreation/startup/webocreation|event'));
        }
    }
    public function event(string &$route, array &$args, mixed &$output): void
    {
        $override = [
            'common/header',
        ];
        if (in_array($route, $override)) {
            $route = 'extension/webocreation/' . $route;
        }
    }
}
```

This overrides the header of the code.

Frontend Template header.twig file of custom Opencart 4 theme

Now, let's create the header.twig at the extension folder, extension >> webocreation >> catalog >> view >> template >> common >> header.twig. Add the following lines of code:

```
<!DOCTYPE html>
<html dir="{{ direction }}" lang="{{ lang }}">
<head>
 <meta charset="UTF-8"/>
 <meta name="viewport" content="width=device-width, initial-scale=1">
 <meta http-equiv="X-UA-Compatible" content="IE=edge">
 <title>{{ title }}</title>
 <base href="{{ base }}"/>
 {% if description %}
        <meta name="description" content="{{ description }}"/>
 {% endif %}
 {% if keywords %}
        <meta name="keywords" content="{{ keywords }}"/>
 {% endif %}
 <script src="{{ jquery }}" type="text/javascript"></script>
 <link href="{{ bootstrap }}" type="text/css" rel="stylesheet" media="screen"/>
 <link href="{{ icons }}" type="text/css" rel="stylesheet"/>
 <link href="{{ stylesheet }}" type="text/css" rel="stylesheet"/>
 <link href="extension/webocreation/catalog/view/stylesheet/stylesheet.css" type="text/css" rel="stylesheet"/>
 {% for style in styles %}
```

```
        <link href="{{ style.href }}" type="text/css" rel="{{ style.rel }}" media="{{ style.media }}"/>
{% endfor %}
{% for script in scripts %}
        <script src="{{ script }}" type="text/javascript"></script>
{% endforconsidering thatjavascript/common.js" type="text/javascript"></script>
{% for link in links %}
        <link href="{{ link.href }}" rel="{{ link.rel }}"/>
{% endfor %}
{% for analytic in analytics %}
        {{ analytic }}
{% endfor %}
</head>
<body>
<nav id="top">
  <div id="alert" class="position-fixed top-0 end-0 p-3" style="z-index: 9999;"></div>
  <div class="container">
        <div class="nav float-start">
        <ul class="list-inline">
        <li class="list-inline-item">{{ currency }}</li>
        <li class="list-inline-item">{{ language }}</li>
        </ul>
        </div>
        <div class="nav float-end">
        <ul class="list-inline">
        <li class="list-inline-item"><a href="{{ contact }}"><i class="fas fa-phone"></i></a> <span class="d-none d-md-inline">{{ telephone }}</span></li>
        <li class="list-inline-item">
        <div class="dropdown">
        <a href="{{ account }}" class="dropdown-toggle" data-bs-toggle="dropdown"><i class="fas fa-user"></i><span class="d-none d-md-inline">{{ text_account }}</span> <i class="fas fa-caret-down"></i></a>
        <ul class="dropdown-menu dropdown-menu-right">
        {% if not logged %}
        <li><a href="{{ register }}" class="dropdown-item">{{ text_register }}</a></li>
        <li><a href="{{ login }}" class="dropdown-item">{{ text_login }}</a></li>
        {% else %}
        <li><a href="{{ account }}" class="dropdown-item">{{ text_account }}</a></li>
        <li><a href="{{ order }}" class="dropdown-item">{{ text_order }}</a></li>
        <li><a href="{{ transaction }}" class="dropdown-item">{{ text_transaction }}</a></li>
        <li><a href="{{ download }}" class="dropdown-item">{{ text_download }}</a></li>
        <li><a href="{{ logout }}" class="dropdown-item">{{ text_logout }}</a></li>
        {% endif %}
        </ul>
        </div>
        </li>
        <li class="list-inline-item"><a href="{{ wishlist }}" id="wishlist-total" title="{{ text_wishlist }}"><i
```

87

```
class="fas fa-heart"></i> <span class="d-none d-md-inline">{{ text_wishlist }}</span></a></li>
        <li class="list-inline-item"><a href="{{ shopping_cart }}" title="{{ text_shopping_cart }}"><i class="fas fa-
shopping-cart"></i> <span class="d-none d-md-inline">{{ text_shopping_cart }}</span></a></li>
        <li class="list-inline-item"><a href="{{ checkout }}" title="{{ text_checkout }}"><i class="fas fa-
share"></i> <span class="d-none d-md-inline">{{ text_checkout }}</span></a></li>
        </ul>
        </div>
    </div>
</nav>
<header>
  <div class="container">
        <div class="row">
        <div class="col-md-3 col-lg-4">
        <div id="logo">
        {% if logo %}
        <a href="{{ home }}"><img src="{{ logo }}" title="{{ name }}" alt="{{ name }}" class="img-
fluid"/></a>
        {% else %}
        <h1><a href="{{ home }}">{{ name }}</a></h1>
        {% endif %}
        </div>
        </div>
        <div class="col-md-5">{{ search }}</div>
        <div id="header-cart" class="col-md-4 col-lg-3">{{ cart }}</div>
        </div>
    </div>
</header>
<main>
  {{ menu }}
```

The above code is similar to the default header code of the core Opencart code, one change is we add the custom stylesheet like below:

```
<link href="extension/webocreation/catalog/view/stylesheet/stylesheet.css" type="text/css" rel="stylesheet"/>
```

There are events to change the stylesheet but for now, we directly add the code like above. Now let's create the stylesheet.css extension >> webocreation >> catalog >> view >> stylesheet >>stylesheet.css. Paste the following code:

```
a {
 color: #f45511;
}
#menu {
 background-color: #f45511;
 background-image: linear-gradient(to bottom, #f45511, #f45511);
 background-repeat: repeat-x;
 border: 1px solid #f45511;
 border-color: #f45511;
 min-height: 40px;
 border-radius: 4px;
```

```
}
.btn-primary {
  color: #ffffff;
  text-shadow: none;
  background-image: linear-gradient(to bottom, #f45511, #f45511);
  background-repeat: repeat-x;
  border-color: #f45511;
}
```

With these codes, your custom Opencart 4 theme is ready, now you can add your CSS as per your requirement and make the website unique. Once it is active, it looks like the below, you can see the demo of the Opencart 4 custom theme

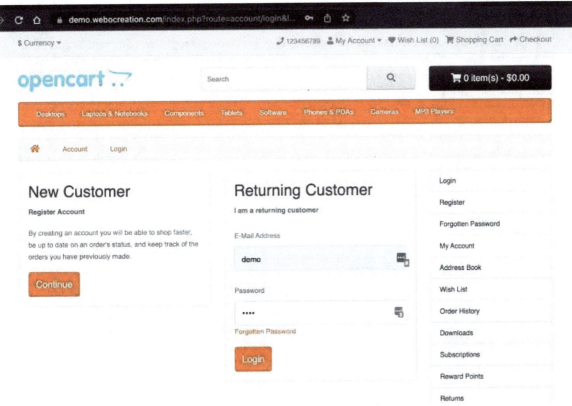

Fig: 8.6

In this way, we complete a simple Opencart 4 theme development tutorial, and you can develop a new custom Opencart 4 theme and change the style, and show it on the front of Opencart 4

9. OPENCART 4 CUSTOM PAGE

In this chapter, we are showing you how to create an additional custom page in my Opencart 4 website by coding. We are showing you by creating the categories listing custom pages in Opencart 4.0.2.3.

 "Opencart Theme and Module Development" book says "Opencart is an e-commerce shopping cart application built with its in-house framework which uses MVCL (Model, view, controller, and language) pattern. Thus, each module in Opencart also follows the MVCL pattern. The controller creates logic and gathers data from the model and it passes data to display in the view." So to create a custom page, we will need a few files for it to work as a page.

The required files are a controller file and a template file. Optional files are the Model file and Language file

Before you start reading below first, understand the request and response in Opencart mentioned in Chapter 2. *For bigger image visit* *https://webocreation.com/opencart-mvcl-flow*

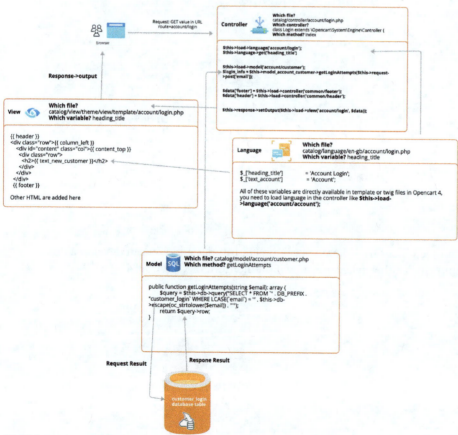

Fig: 9.1

Creating a custom page in OpenCart 4 allows you to extend your store's functionality and provide additional information or services to your customers. Whether you want to create a custom information page, a landing page for a promotion, or any other specific content, OpenCart makes it relatively easy to add and manage custom pages. We'll walk you through the steps needed to create a custom page in OpenCart 4.

Create the Controller

The first step is to create a new controller for your custom page. The controller will handle the logic and data needed for the page. Navigate to the catalog/controller directory in your OpenCart installation and create a new folder named custom. Inside this folder, create a new PHP file named custom.php. Just for simple test, let's add the following code in the custom.php file:

```php
<?php
namespace Opencart\Catalog\Controller\Custom;
/**
 * Class Custom
 *
 * @package Opencart\Catalog\Controller\Custom
 */
class Custom extends \Opencart\System\Engine\Controller {
    /**
     * @return ?\Opencart\System\Engine\Action
     */
    public function index(): ?\Opencart\System\Engine\Action {
        echo "We are here";
        return null;
    }
}
```

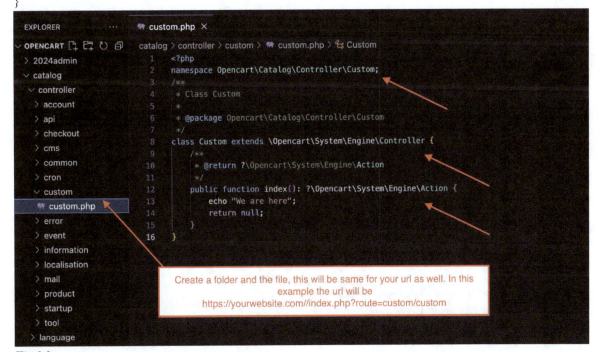

Fig: 9.2

This code is for you to show the URL and how the index gives you the output. Now go to https://yourwebsite.com/index.php?route=custom/custom then you will see the output like below, our local URL is opencart.loc:

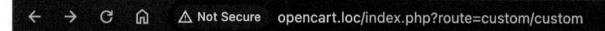

We are here

Fig: 9.3

Let's improve the controller a little bit more.

Define the Controller Class:

Open the custom.php file remove the above code and add following code:

```php
<?php
namespace Opencart\Catalog\Controller\Custom;
/**
 * Class Custom
 *
 * @package Opencart\Catalog\Controller\Custom
 */
class Custom extends \Opencart\System\Engine\Controller {
    /**
     * @return ?\Opencart\System\Engine\Action
     */
    public function index(): void {
        $this->load->language('custom/custom');
        $this->document->setTitle($this->language->get('heading_title'));
        $data['breadcrumbs'] = [];
        $data['breadcrumbs'][] = [
            'text' => $this->language->get('text_home'),
            'href' => $this->url->link('common/home', 'language=' . $this->config->get('config_language'))
        ];
        $data['breadcrumbs'][] = [
            'text' => $this->language->get('heading_title'),
            'href' => $this->url->link('custom/custom', 'language=' . $this->config->get('config_language'))
        ];
        $data['column_left'] = $this->load->controller('common/column_left');
        $data['column_right'] = $this->load->controller('common/column_right');
        $data['content_top'] = $this->load->controller('common/content_top');
        $data['content_bottom'] = $this->load->controller('common/content_bottom');
        $data['footer'] = $this->load->controller('common/footer');
        $data['header'] = $this->load->controller('common/header');
        $this->response->setOutput($this->load->view('custom/custom', $data));
    }
```

92

```
}
```

Nothing fancy here, but whatever data you passed from the controller in $data['YOURVARIABLE'], you have access to the YOURVARIABLE in the template twig file and just output as {{ YOURVARIABLE }}. This way you build logic in the controller, get the desired results, assign it to the $data array, and send it to the template. Whatever you define here, it will access the template twig file when you load a file in the controller. Now let's change the /catalog/controller/catalog/custom.php like below:

This is how we load the language files in the controller:

$this->load->language('custom/custom');

Then we can use the language file variable in the controller and language file. In the controller, we use the language variable like

$this->document->setTitle($this->language->get('heading_title'));

In the template twig file that is rendered by the controller, we can use directly with {{LANGUAGEVARIABLE}}, so our catalog/theme/view/THEMENAME/template/catalog/custom.twig can directly access to categories_text variable of the language file. Please be careful you can directly access the language variable in the twig file in Opencart 3 and above, in Opencart 2 you cannot directly access it without assigning it to the $data variable in the controller.

As we write in our code *$this->response->setOutput($this->load->view('custom/custom', $data));*, it means we are outputting code in custom.twig file at catalog/theme/view/default/template/custom/custom.twig.

Create the Language File

Next, create a language file to store the text strings for your custom page. Navigate to the catalog/language/en-gb directory and create a new folder named custom. Inside this folder, create a file named custom.php. Open the custom.php file and add the following code:

```
<?php
// Text
$_['heading_title'] = 'Custom Page';
$_['text_error'] = 'Custom Page Not Found!';
```

Create a View File

The view file defines the HTML structure of your custom page. Navigate to the catalog/view/theme/default/template directory and create a new folder named custom. Inside this folder, create a file named custom.twig. Open the custom.twig file and add the following code:

```
{{ header }}
<div class="container">
  <ul class="breadcrumb">
    {% for breadcrumb in breadcrumbs %}
    <li class="breadcrumb-item"><a href="{{ breadcrumb.href }}">{{ breadcrumb.text }}</a></li>
    {% endfor %}
  </ul>
```

```
<div class="row">{{ column_left }}
  <div id="content" class="col">{{ content_top }}
    <h1>{{ heading_title }}</h1>
    <div>
    You can add anything you want here
    </div>
  {{ column_right }}
  </div>
</div>
{{ footer }}
```

Access Your Custom Page

Finally, access your custom page by navigating to the following URL in your browser:
http://yourstore.com/index.php?route=custom/custom Replace yourstore.com with the actual URL of your OpenCart store.

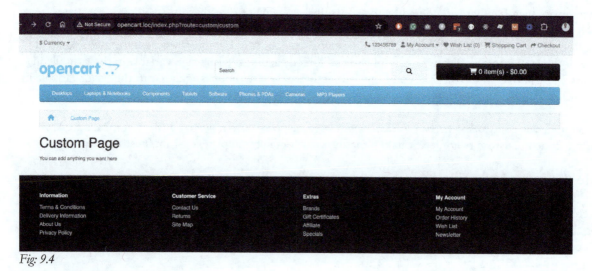

Fig: 9.4

Debugging

If you get an error like the one below don't panic just go to Admin >> Extensions >> Modifications and click the Refresh button.

Fatal error: Uncaught Error: Class Custom not found in …/modification/system/engine/action.php:71 Stack trace: #0 ../catalog/controller/startup/router.php(25): Action->execute(Object(Registry)) #1 …/modification/system/engine/action.php(79): ControllerStartupRouter->index() #2 /system/engine/router.php(67): Action->execute(Object(Registry)) #3 /system/engine/router.php(56): Router->execute(Object(Action)) #4 /system/framework.php(165): Router->dispatch(Object(Action), Object(Action)) #5 system/startup.php(104): require_once('/Applications/X…') #6 /index.php(19): start('catalog') #7 {main} thrown in **modification/system/engine/action.php** *on line 71*

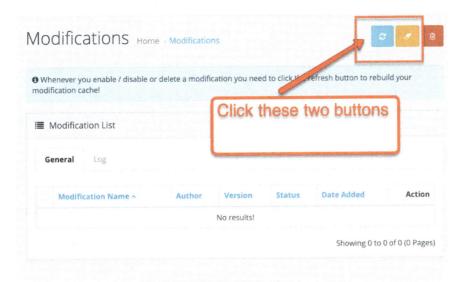

Fig: 9.5

If you don't see the page as per your design, it means you have not cleared the theme cache and SCSS cache, which you can do from the admin dashboard:

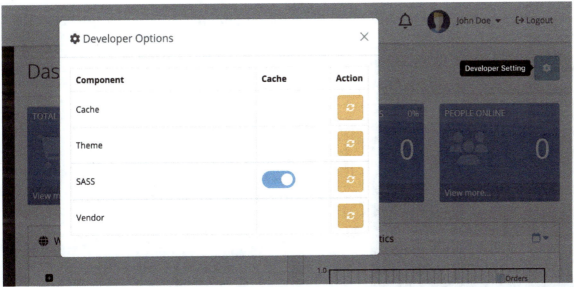

Fig: 9.6

10. OPENCART 4 CUSTOM LANGUAGE

Opencart supports multi-language. In Opencart 4, language is also an extension. We can add a new language in Opencart 4 and we can configure it to set it as a default language other than English. Adding a custom language to your OpenCart 4 store allows you to reach a broader audience and cater to customers who speak different languages. OpenCart's flexible language management system makes it easy to add and configure new languages. While working with language extension, you need a country flag which you can download the small size flag from https://github.com/rupaknepali/Opencart-free-modules/raw/master/backupZipFolder/flags.zip. You also need a language code which you can find in the lists of ISO 639-1 Language Codes at W3Schools. https://www.w3schools.com/tags/ref_language_codes.asp OpenCart tries to detect the language your browser is using even if the database is down it will use the directory name to see. The language directory should be named after Web browser language identification codes in lowercase.

File and folder structure of custom language for Opencart 4

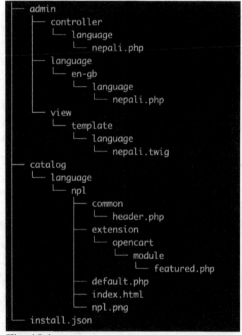

Fig: 10.1

install.json As with every extension, the language extension also has install.json where you can enter the details in JSON.

catalog >> language >> npl is the folder where we will add all the language files. As per Fig 10.1, we are translating default.php, common/header.php, and featured extension languages. **npl.png** is the flag image of

Nepal.

The **Admin folder** contains all the installation code and if you want to change the language of the admin section then you need to add the respective folders in the language. In the above example, we just want to change the language in the catalog folder, so all the language text will be in the common header (catalog/language/npl/common/header.php), similarly, we'll walk you through the steps to create and integrate a custom language into your OpenCart 4 store.

Prepare the Language Pack

To create a custom language, you need to prepare a language pack containing the translated text for all the language files used in OpenCart. You will be creating "Nepalese" or "Nepali" as a new language as there is no language pack for Nepal country language. To start, let's create a folder called **nepali/** and inside it create an install.json file and paste the following code, if you are making your own language pack enter your details as necessary.

Create an install.json

```
{
  "name": "Nepali Language",
  "description": "Nepali language for OpenCart.",
  "version": "1.0",
  "author": "Webocreation",
  "link": "https://webocreation.com"
}
```

Create a Language file of Admin section

Inside the nepali/ folder create an admin/ folder and then inside the admin/ folder create language/ folder, inside the language/ folder create en-gb/ folder and inside it create nepali.php file and paste following code:

```php
<?php
// Heading
$_['heading_title']    = 'Nepali Language';
// Text
$_['text_extension']   = 'Extensions';
$_['text_success']     = 'Success: You have modified Nepali language!';
$_['text_edit']        = 'Edit the Nepali Language';
// Entry
$_['entry_status']     = 'Status';
// Error
$_['error_permission'] = 'Warning: You do not have permission to modify Nepali language!';
```

The code above is a language file for installing the language extension and configuring it. Now let's create the controller of the admin section

Create Controller of the Admin section

Inside the nepali/ folder create an admin/ folder and then inside the admin/ folder create controller/, inside controller/ create language/ folder, inside the language/ folder create nepali.php file and paste following code. These codes have logic to create breadcrumbs, set links like save, and back in the data, set form field values, and set variables like header, footer, etc controller and pass that data to the view, similarly have code to add new language in the database when installed, remove the language from a database table.

```php
<?php
namespace Opencart\Admin\Controller\Extension\Nepali\Language;
class Nepali extends \Opencart\System\Engine\Controller {
    public function index(): void {
        $this->load->language('extension/nepali/language/nepali');
        $this->document->setTitle($this->language->get('heading_title'));
        $data['breadcrumbs'] = [];
        $data['breadcrumbs'][] = [
            'text' => $this->language->get('text_home'),
            'href' => $this->url->link('common/dashboard', 'user_token=' . $this->session->data['user_token'])
        ];
        $data['breadcrumbs'][] = [
            'text' => $this->language->get('text_extension'),
            'href' => $this->url->link('marketplace/extension', 'user_token=' . $this->session->data['user_token'] .
'&type=language')
        ];
        $data['breadcrumbs'][] = [
            'text' => $this->language->get('heading_title'),
            'href' => $this->url->link('extension/nepali/language/nepali', 'user_token=' . $this->session->data['user_token'])
        ];
        $data['save'] = $this->url->link('extension/nepali/language/nepali.save', 'user_token=' . $this->session-
>data['user_token']);
        $data['back'] = $this->url->link('marketplace/extension', 'user_token=' . $this->session->data['user_token'] .
'&type=language');
        $data['language_nepali_status'] = $this->config->get('language_nepali_status');
        $data['header'] = $this->load->controller('common/header');
        $data['column_left'] = $this->load->controller('common/column_left');
        $data['footer'] = $this->load->controller('common/footer');
        $this->response->setOutput($this->load->view('extension/nepali/language/nepali', $data));
    }
    public function save(): void {
        $this->load->language('extension/nepali/language/nepali');
        $json = [];
        if (!$this->user->hasPermission('modify', 'extension/nepali/language/nepali')) {
            $json['error'] = $this->language->get('error_permission');
        }
        if (!$json) {
            $this->load->model('setting/setting');
            $this->model_setting_setting->editSetting('language_nepali', $this->request->post);
            $json['success'] = $this->language->get('text_success');
        }
        $this->response->addHeader('Content-Type: application/json');
```

```php
        $this->response->setOutput(json_encode($json));
    }
    public function install(): void {
        if ($this->user->hasPermission('modify', 'extension/language')) {
            $language_info = $this->model_localisation_language->getLanguageByCode('npl');
            if (!$language_info) {
                $language_data = [
                    'name'       => 'Nepali',
                    'code'       => 'npl',
                    'locale'     => 'npl',
                    'extension'  => 'nepali',
                    'status'     => 1,
                    'sort_order' => 1
                ];
                $this->load->model('localisation/language');
                $this->model_localisation_language->addLanguage($language_data);
            } else {
                $this->load->model('localisation/language');
                $this->model_localisation_language->editLanguage($language_info['language_id'], $language_info + ['extension'
=> 'nepali']);
            }
        }
    }
    public function uninstall(): void {
        if ($this->user->hasPermission('modify', 'extension/language')) {
            $this->load->model('localisation/language');
            $language_info = $this->model_localisation_language->getLanguageByCode('npl');
            if ($language_info) {
                $this->model_localisation_language->deleteLanguage($language_info['language_id']);
            }
        }
    }
}
```

Here are some explanation of some code:
As mentioned the Admin namespace can be named as
*namespace Opencart\Admin\Controller\Extension**ExtensionFolderName\ExtensionType;***
That is why its namespace is like below because its extension folder name is nepali and extension type is
language. *namespace Opencart\Admin\Controller\Extension\Nepali\Language;*

The filename is nepali.php so the class name is Nepali, it should always extend the
\Opencart\System\Engine\Controller.

class Nepali extends \Opencart\System\Engine\Controller {

In this example we have four methods index(), save(), install(), and uninstall(), you can have any methods as
per your business requirements or logic. In most of the extensions, they need to have a setting page for

configuration so index() is to load everything, and save() is to save the form data. You can see the install() method which is called automatically when a module is installed as we need to add a new language in the database oc_language table which will show at Admin >> System >> Localization >> Languages. Likewise, there is an uninstall() method which is also called automatically when the language extension is uninstalled, which will remove the language from the database oc_language table.

index() method

Quick tips: everything in this method is similar, you can just change the nepali to your language name and you should be set. Other codes are already defined so hope you already know most of them. Just to highlight, this code line is for the form status field which will set the status in the oc_setting database table gets it and set the value to the data array.

$data['language_nepali_status'] = $this->config->get('language_nepali_status');

install() method

This install method is called when someone clicks the install button of the Nepali language at Admin >> Extensions >> Extensions >> Filter extension type as Language and click the Install button of Nepali language.

Languages

Language Name	Status		Action
Nepali Language	Disabled		✏ ➕

Fig: 10.2

$language_info = $this->model_localisation_language->getLanguageByCode('npl'); This is to get the language as per the code. Here the code is npl, you can change to your language code. The logic here is to try to get from the database oc_language table and see if the values exist, if not then add the new language. To add first we set the language information like in this variable:

```
$language_data = [
  'name'      => 'Nepali',
  'code'      => 'npl',
  'locale'    => 'npl',
  'extension' => 'nepali',
  'status'    => 1,
  'sort_order' => 1
];
```

Change the above as per your language.

Language Name: We can give any name but better to give a lexical name as this is shown in the front end of the store. For our example, we gave it "Nepali)".

Code: The code is auto-selected and shown in the dropdown. The ISO language code can be found at https://www.w3schools.com/tags/ref_language_codes.asp

Locale: Browsers use Locale to auto-detect the language so we need to enter as per the browser standard which we can find at https://developer.chrome.com/webstore/i18n#localeTable

Extension: Extension name that you will be uploading, for simplicity you can keep the language name.

Status: To enable the language at the front select Enabled.

Sort Order: This is the order to show the languages in front of the dropdown.

Then, the code below will add that language info to the oc_language database table:

$this->load->model('localisation/language');

$this->model_localisation_language->addLanguage($language_data);

If you see the oc_language database table, you will see data like below image:

language_id	name	code	locale	extension	sort_order	status
1	English	en-gb	en-gb,en	*NULL*	1	1
8	Nepali	npl	npl	nepali	1	1

Fig: 10.3

In this way, the language install method works.

Uninstall() method

This uninstall method is called when someone clicks the uninstall button of the Nepali language at Admin >> Extensions >> Extensions >> Filter extension type as Language and click the Uninstall button of Nepali language.

$language_info = $this->model_localisation_language->getLanguageByCode('npl');

if ($language_info) {

   $this->model_localisation_language->deleteLanguage($language_info['language_id']);

}

Create View of Admin section

Inside the extension/nepali/ folder create an admin/ folder and then inside admin/ folder create view/, inside view/ create template/ folder, inside the template/ folder create language/ folder and inside the language/ folder create file called nepali.twig and paste following code.

```
{{ header }}{{ column_left }}
<div id="content">
  <div class="page-header">
    <div class="container-fluid">
      <div class="float-end">
        <button type="submit" form="form-language" data-bs-toggle="tooltip" title="{{ button_save }}" class="btn btn-primary"><i class="fas fa-save"></i></button>
        <a href="{{ back }}" data-bs-toggle="tooltip" title="{{ button_back }}" class="btn btn-light"><i class="fas fa-reply"></i></a></div>
      <h1>{{ heading_title }}</h1>
      <ol class="breadcrumb">
        {% for breadcrumb in breadcrumbs %}
        <li class="breadcrumb-item"><a href="{{ breadcrumb.href }}">{{ breadcrumb.text }}</a></li>
        {% endfor %}
      </ol>
    </div>
```

```
</div>
<div class="container-fluid">
  <div class="card">
    <div class="card-header"><i class="fas fa-pencil-alt"></i> {{ text_edit }}</div>
    <div class="card-body">
      <form id="form-language" action="{{ save }}" method="post" data-oc-toggle="ajax">
        <div class="row mb-3">
          <label class="col-sm-2 col-form-label">{{ entry_status }}</label>
          <div class="col-sm-10">
            <div class="form-check form-switch form-switch-lg">
              <input type="checkbox" name="language_nepali_status" value="1" id="input-status" class="form-check-input"{% if language_nepali_status %} checked{% endif %}/>
            </div>
          </div>
        </div>
      </form>
    </div>
  </div>
</div>
</div>
{{ footer }}
```

With the above code in view file the output is like in the image below:

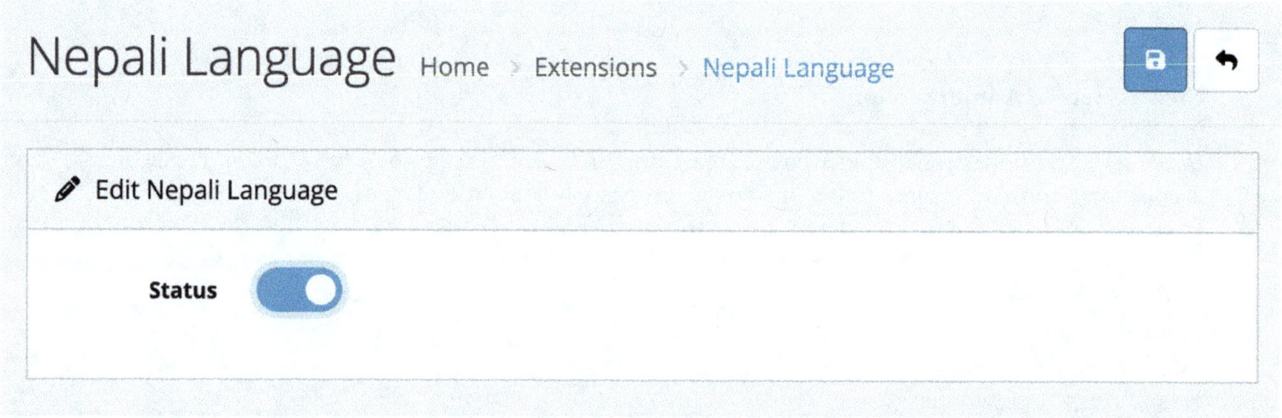

Fig: 10.4

Others are self-explanatory, only below checkbox code need the name to always start with language_

`<input type="checkbox" name="language_nepali_status" value="1" id="input-status" class="form-check-input"{% if language_nepali_status %} checked{% endif %}/>`

In this way, your Nepali language form is ready, from where you can enable the status of Nepali language. Activate the Status checkbox and save. With this, the Nepali language is ready to show in the front end.

Create Catalog section

For the front-end, go to nepali/ folder, create a catalog/ folder, inside the catalog/ folder create language/ folder, inside the language folder create npl/folder, in that npl/ folder create default.php and add a small Nepal flag logo with name same as code npl.png. Open default.php and add the following code $_['code'] to your locale for Nepali it is npl.

```
<?php
// Locale
$_['code']              = 'npl';
$_['direction']         = 'ltr';
$_['date_format_short']   = 'd.m.Y';
$_['date_format_long']    = 'l j. F Y';
$_['time_format']       = 'H:i:s';
$_['datetime_format']     = 'd.m.Y H:i:s';
$_['decimal_point']       = ',';
$_['thousand_point']      = '.';
// Text
$_['text_yes']          = 'हुन्छ';
$_['button_cart']           = 'भाडोमा हाल्नुस्';
```

With the above default.php change and Nepali language is active, you can see the button_cart changed the 'Add to cart' to 'भाडोमा हाल्नुस्'

Fig: 10.5

With this your language extension is ready to be used, only remaining is to translate all the text to your language.

Translate the Files

To translate all the files, go to catalog/language/en-gb and copy all the folders account, API, checkout, etc, and go to nepali/catalog/language/npl and paste all those folders and then you can open files inside all folders and start converting to your language. Example of a translated language Open each and every ***.php and change English text to your language text except the variable in $_['DONTCHANGE']. For example, if you open catalog/language/np/default.php then you need to change the

$_['text_yes'] = 'Yes';

to

$_['text_yes'] = 'हुन्छ';

Just change values after the equal sign. Do the same for all of the other files.

You need to translate for other extensions as well, so for that go to extension >> opencart >> catalog >> language >> en-gb and copy all the folders, then go to extension >> nepali >> extension >> opencart and paste all the folders and translate all the files to your language.

If you are looking to translate the admin section then you need to do the same, go to admin >> language >> en-gb and copy all the folders, and then go to extension >> nepali >> admin >> language >> npl >> language and paste all the folders and translate all the files to your language.

Zipping and naming language extension

Once all files are translated, go inside the nepali/folder and then zip all the files, you should be inside the nepali folder. Then name it as nepali.ocmod.zip.

Again, Don't zip the nepali/ folder, go inside the nepali/ folder and zip all admin/, catalog/, and install.json. We see people zipping the folder instead of going inside the folder and zipping the files and folders.

Upload a new language pack in Opencart 4

Find your language pack at Opencart Marketplace. Then download any language pack, for demo purposes. Once you click the download button if you are not logged then it redirects to the login page else it will show the download section. Download the right version. You will get a zip file like "***.ocmod.zip**". Now go to admin >> Extensions >> Installer >> click Upload and select the zip file you just downloaded "***.ocmod.zip". After you see the upload success message, go to admin >> Extensions >> Extensions >> Choose extension type Language >> then install language

Go to Admin>>Extensions>> Modifications and click the refresh button at the top right corner.

Test Your Custom Language

After setting up your custom language, it's crucial to test it to ensure everything works correctly. On the front end of your store, use the language selector to switch to your custom language. Browse through different pages to check if the translations appear correctly. If you set the admin language to your custom language, navigate through the admin panel to verify the translations. You can see the dropdown of languages like the below image when you add the new language, we added the Nepali language, and now you can see like below:

Fig: 10.6

Change the default language of Opencart 4

To change the default language to another language, go to admin >> System >>Settings >> Edit the store. Click the Local tab and select the Language, and Administration Language to the preferred language.

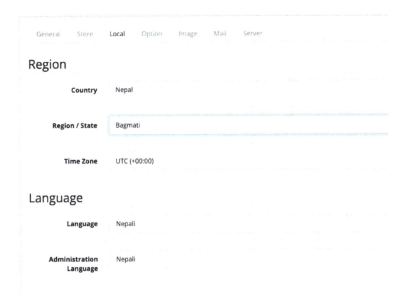

Fig: 10.7

Override the language texts from Admin Interface

Opencart 4 provides an easy admin interface to override the language texts of any languages that are already added. For that go to Admin >> Design >> Language Editor and then click the add button, then you will see the form below, where you can choose which Language, which Route, and which key, then change the value. In the example, we are changing "Email Address" in the login form to "Please enter your Email Address"

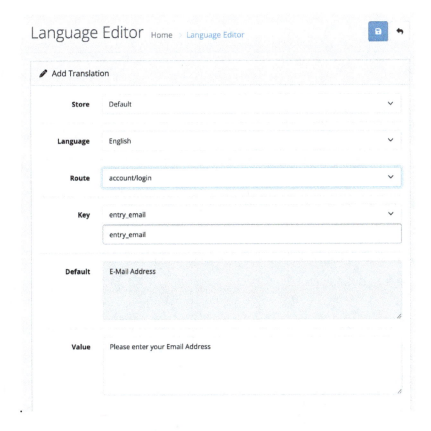

Fig: 10.8

Now go to the login page and you will see the Email Address changed like below:

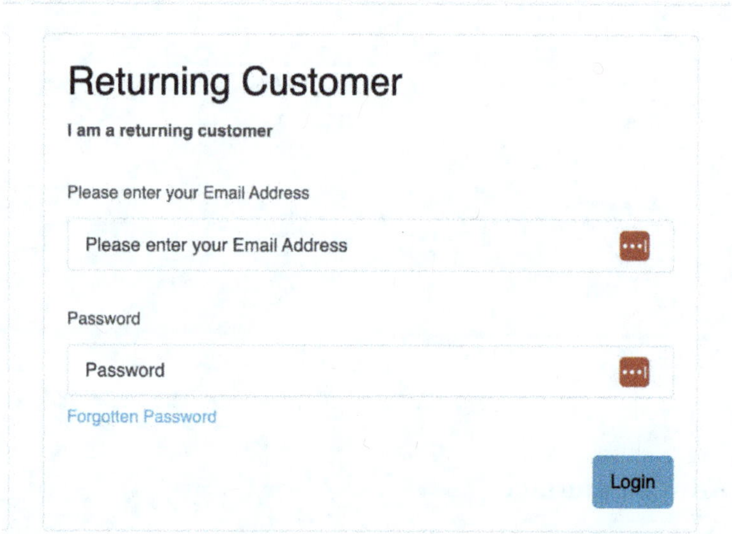

Returning Customer

I am a returning customer

Please enter your Email Address

Please enter your Email Address

Password

Password

Forgotten Password

Login

Fig: 10.9

In this way, you can create a custom language extension, upload a new language, install the new language in Opencart 4, show it in front of the store, set the different default languages other than English, and override the language as well.

11. OPENCART API DOCUMENTATION

The OpenCart 4 APIs allow developers to manage store data, including products, orders, customers, and categories, through RESTful endpoints. Each application that uses the API will have to go through a couple of steps to register, authorize the user, and work with the API. Operations include:

- create — Creates with the specified parameters.
  For example, you can add products to the cart as given by Opencart API post request of products or product_id at /index.php?route=api/cart/add
- read — Retrieves information about the specified object.
  For example, you can retrieve the shipping methods with the endpoint:
  index.php?route=api/shipping/methods
- query — Retrieves objects that match specified criteria.
- update — Updates elements of an existing object.
- upsert — Updates elements of an existing object if it exists. If the object does not exist, one is created using the supplied parameters.

Developers must authenticate with the API before issuing requests. Some considerations must be taken while performing requests. When performing update requests, only the fields specified in the request are updated, and all others are left unchanged. If a required field is cleared during an update, the request will be declined.

Base URL: The base URL for the API is: http://yourstore.com/index.php?route=api/ Replace yourstore.com with the URL of your OpenCart store.

Create API username and key

Login requests that meet these criteria will be granted an api_token id. You can get the API username and API key from:

- Log in to your OpenCart admin panel.
- Navigate to System > Users > API.
- Click on the Add New button or edit an existing API user.
- Ensure the API user status is set to Enabled.
- Click on the Generate button next to the API Key field.
- Add IP address from where you want to call these API calls. If you want to call from anywhere then you can enter *.*.*.*
- Save the API user.
- Both the Username and API key are unique to individual users. **API Token ID is valid for 60 minutes.** In contrast, user keys are valid indefinitely which you can regenerate as needed.

Opencart user, permissions, user group management, and API users

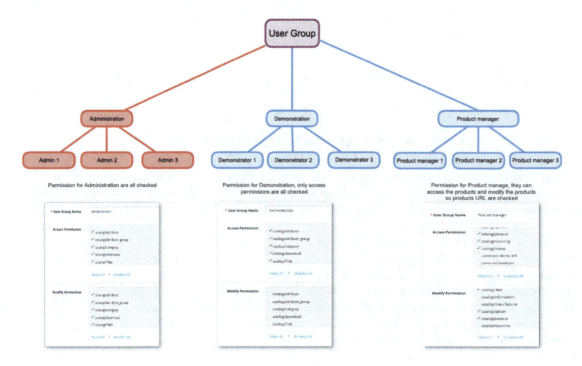

Fig: 11.1

To manage the Opencart admin section, Opencart can have multiple users with different user groups and each user group can have different permissions for the management of Opencart stores. The powerful user group is the Administrator by default but you can change it as per your requirement. For users, user groups, and permissions management, go to Admin >> System >> Users where you will see as below in the left menu:

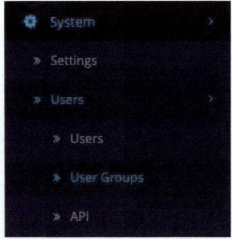

Fig: 11.2

First, go to Admin >> System >> Users >> User Groups where you can see by default installation Administrator and Demonstration, edit Administrator and you will see like below:

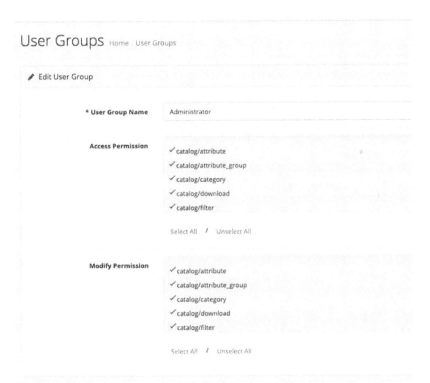

Fig: 11.3

As the Administrator is a superuser, everything is checked. Be sure to whom you are making the Administrator user. There are two permissions: Access Permission and Modify Permission. With Access permission, the user can see the page which is checked. With Modify permission, the user can edit the section which is checked.

How to identify the page for permission in Opencart?

In Access Permission and Modify the permission on the right side you see the checkbox which is the parts of the URL and the route of the page. Like:

https://YOURURL/admin/index.php?route=**catalog/category**&user_token=***

In the above URL after the **route=** you see **catalog/category** which is the one you will see on the right side of the access and modify permission. So you can now find your URL and decide how to give permissions to the

Authentication and Request Format of Opencart API:

OpenCart API uses token-based authentication. You need to generate an API token to make authenticated requests. Authentication requests sent to the Opencart API URL:

1. It must be made via SSL encrypted connection
2. Must use HTTP POST
3. Must contain username and key for the Opencart user account that will be submitting API requests

Request

POST /index.php?route=api/login

Request Parameters

Parameter	Required	Description
username	yes	The API username
key	yes	The API keys generated for the API user

CURL login example:

Let's say Opencart is hosted at *demo.webocreation.com* and you like to login through API from different websites, let's say rupaknepali.com.np then you can use the following CURL login code in the rupaknepali.com.np, in this example the username is rupak and key is *KcekZLhYEH2Y6fLpfNm4dK2XuJJ7vnwWC0ugRW1P8fPnfu1lQxjwSAcjXFda1Ma46l25E6cIiwyO5bZ1oGfLwz2 T13Q2qE0yBw10DL2H7DCWefaJghEkvhiVH2gg6zJ5XCwdseMCaQPQEw1VVs6QM0v56RdlZBcxhsqS7OaLXJ urZhA73JRmTOD7Q4eMGnLrsjQUHFtrKaFkmV3UeLqkg1T3FfapFsHYh7nHvV4ec1elumNYP6g0BW6c1*

```php
<?php
$curl = curl_init();
curl_setopt_array($curl, array(
  CURLOPT_URL => 'https://demo.webocreation.com/index.php?route=api%2Faccount%2Flogin&language=en-gb&store_id=0',
  CURLOPT_RETURNTRANSFER => true,
  CURLOPT_ENCODING => '',
  CURLOPT_MAXREDIRS => 10,
  CURLOPT_TIMEOUT => 0,
  CURLOPT_FOLLOWLOCATION => true,
  CURLOPT_HTTP_VERSION => CURL_HTTP_VERSION_1_1,
  CURLOPT_CUSTOMREQUEST => 'POST',
  CURLOPT_POSTFIELDS => array('username' => 'rupak','key' =>
'KcekZLhYEH2Y6fLpfNm4dK2XuJJ7vnwWC0ugRW1P8fPnfu1lQxjwSAcjXFda1Ma46l25E6cIiwyO5bZ1oGfLwz2
T13Q2qE0yBw10DL2H7DCWefaJghEkvhiVH2gg6zJ5XCwdseMCaQPQEw1VVs6QM0v56RdlZBcxhsqS7OaLXJ
urZhA73JRmTOD7Q4eMGnLrsjQUHFtrKaFkmV3UeLqkg1T3FfapFsHYh7nHvV4ec1elumNYP6g0BW6c1'),
  CURLOPT_HTTPHEADER => array(
    'Cookie: OCSESSID=1f0e618b2db32e0f1c9c2093c5; currency=USD'
  ),
));
$response = curl_exec($curl);
curl_close($curl);
echo $response;
```

If we pasted above CURL code in api.php and upload in the root folder of http://rupaknepali.com.np, then when we access the https://rupaknepali.com.np/api.php then we will see output like below:

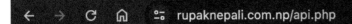

{"success":"Success: API session successfully started!","api_token":"8d575d1e28776ceb16e2dd8279"}

Fig: 11.4

If authentication is successful, a 32-character hexadecimal API token and success message will be returned in the following format:

{"success":"Success: API session successfully started!","api_token":"8d575d1e28776ceb16e2dd8279"}

Include this api_token in the Authorization header for subsequent requests.

Example Curl POST Request in Opencart API:

```
curl -X POST \
 'https://demo.webocreation.com/index.php?route=api%2Faccount%2Flogin&language=en-gb&store_id=0' \
 -H 'cache-control: no-cache' \
 -H 'content-type: application/x-www-form-urlencoded' \
 -H 'postman-token: 2ef6e7f4-84d1-28ae-84b0-ae2dcebeab2f' \
 -d
 'key=KcekZLhYEH2Y6fLpfNm4dK2XuJJ7vnwWC0ugRW1P8fPnfu1lQxjwSAgjXFda1Ma46l25E6cIiwyO5bZ1oGf
 Lwz2T13Q2qE0yBw10DL2H7DCWefaJghEkvhiVH2gg6zJ5XCwdseMCaQPQEw1VVs6QM0v56RdlZBcxhsqS7O
 aLXJurZhA73JRmTOD7Q4eMGnLrsjQUHFtrKaFkmV3UeLqkg1T3FfapFsHYh7nHvV4ec1elumNYP6g0BW6c1
 nzc3hE1&username=rupak'
```

Example curl GET request in Opencart API:

```
curl -X GET \
 'https://demo.webocreation.com/index.php?route=api%2Fsale%2Fcart&api_token=8d575d1e28776ceb16e2dd8279' \
 -H 'cache-control: no-cache' \
 -H 'postman-token: 969b0a8f-aa76-5ec5-10f5-a5f768a2868d'
```

Here api_token=YOUR_TOKEN_VALUE returned from the login. It will give the following results when there are no products:

```
{
  "products": [],
  "vouchers": [],
  "totals": [
    {
      "title": "Sub-Total",
      "text": "$0.00"
    },
    {
```

```
        "title": "Total",
        "text": "$0.00"
     }
   ]
}
```

Opencart 4 API Endpoints

Similarly, you can use the following API endpoints:

index.php?route=api/account/login	POST	username and key
index.php?route=api/localisation/currency	POST	currency
index.php?route=api/sale/affiliate	POST	affiliate_id
/index.php?route=api/sale/cart	POST	
index.php?route=api/sale/cart.add	POST	product_id, quantity, option, subscription_plan_id
index.php?route=api/sale/cart.edit	POST	key, quantity
index.php?route=api/sale/cart.remove	POST	key
index.php?route=api/sale/coupon	POST	coupon
index.php?route=api/sale/customer	POST	customer_id, firstname, lastname, email
index.php?route=api/sale/order.load	GET	order_id
index.php?route=api/sale/order.save	POST	
index.php?route=api/sale/order.comment	POST	comment
index.php?route=api/sale/order.confirm	GEthe T	
index.php?route=api/sale/order.delete	GET/POST	For the post selected, to get order_id
index.php?route=api/sale/order.addHistory	POST	order_id, order_status_id, comment, notify, override
index.php?route=api/sale/payment_address	POST	firstname, lastname, company, address_1, address_2, postcode, city, zone_id, country_id
index.php?route=api/sale/payment_method	GET	
index.php?route=api/sale/payment_method.save	POST	payment_method
index.php?route=api/sale/reward	POST	reward

index.php?route=api/sale/reward.maximum	GET	
index.php?route=api/sale/reward.available	GET	
index.php?route=api/sale/shipping_address	POST	firstname, lastname, company, address_1, address_2, postcode, city, zone_id, country_id
index.php?route=api/sale/shipping_method	GET	
index.php?route=api/sale/shipping_method.save	POST	shipping_address
index.php?route=api/sale/voucher	POST	voucher
index.php?route=api/sale/voucher.add	POST	from_name, from_email, to_name, to_email, voucher_theme_id, message, amount
index.php?route=api/sale/voucher.remove	POST	key

The OpenCart API provides a comprehensive set of endpoints that allow you to interact with your OpenCart store programmatically. With these endpoints, you can authenticate, retrieve, create, and update various resources within your store. Whether you're integrating with third-party applications, developing mobile apps, or building custom extensions, the OpenCart API offers the flexibility and functionality needed.

Postman testing of Opencart 4 endpoints

Postman is an invaluable tool for testing and debugging OpenCart 4 API endpoints. First, you need to log in then only you can perform another call, for login here is the endpoint **/index.php?route=api/account/login,** and for this API call you need a username and key which you can find at admin>> Settings >> Users >> API. Here is the POSTMAN testing:

Fig: 11.5

After this login call, now you can call other endpoints, for that you need to set the cookie with the api_token value.

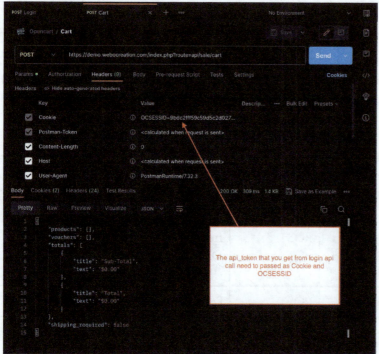

Fig: 11.6

Create custom API endpoints in Opencart 4

Opencart 4 has provided a limited number of API calls so you may need custom API endpoints which we are showing you to develop new ones. We take an example between two servers one from https://demo.webocreation.com which acts as Server Responder of API which is built in Opencart and https://rupaknepali.com.com.np/ as the requestor. For example, if you want an API endpoint that returns all categories then you need to create a custom endpoint.

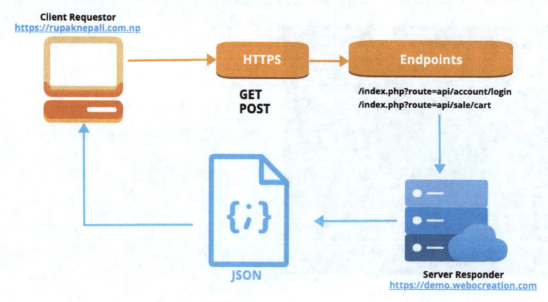

Fig: 11.7

The responding server

Opencart does not provide an API to serve the category by default through API, so we need to make some changes in the responding server to serve all categories. For that in your responding server go to catalog/controller/api/ and create category.php and paste the following lines of code:

```php
<?php
namespace Opencart\Catalog\Controller\Api;
/**
 * Class Category
 * @package Opencart\Catalog\Controller\Api
 */
class Category extends \Opencart\System\Engine\Controller {
    /**
     * @return void
     */
    public function index(): void {
        $json = [];
        $this->load->model('catalog/category');
        $categories = $this->model_catalog_category->getCategories();
        if ($categories) {
            $json['categories'] = $categories;
        } else {
            $json['error'] = 'No Categories';
        }
        $this->response->addHeader('Content-Type: application/json');
        $this->response->setOutput(json_encode($json));
    }
}
```

With the above code it will provide you directly accessing API URL index.php?route=api/category. As per our example, it is https://demo.webocreation.com/index.php?route=api/category.

Requesting server

In your requesting server, create a file let's say apicategory.php, as per our example let's say we create https://rupaknepali.com.np/apicategory.php In this file let's make a CURL request to get the category: https://demo.webocreation.com/index.php?route=api/category. Following is the code:

```php
<?php
$curl = curl_init();
curl_setopt_array($curl, array(
  CURLOPT_URL => 'https://demo.webocreation.com/index.php?route=api%2Fcategory',
  CURLOPT_RETURNTRANSFER => true,
  CURLOPT_ENCODING => '',
  CURLOPT_MAXREDIRS => 10,
  CURLOPT_TIMEOUT => 0,
  CURLOPT_FOLLOWLOCATION => true,
  CURLOPT_HTTP_VERSION => CURL_HTTP_VERSION_1_1,
```

```
CURLOPT_CUSTOMREQUEST => 'GET',
CURLOPT_HTTPHEADER => array(
  'Cookie: OCSESSID=8e2124a292ec606ad4f4e9eac1; currency=USD'
 ),
));
$response = curl_exec($curl);
curl_close($curl);
echo $response;
```

The response you get will be like below:

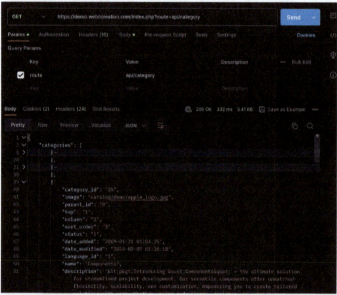

Fig: 11.8

As per our API setup, it just returns all category details. If you want to make changes then you have to make changes in catalog/controller/api/category.php as per your need. In this way, you can retrieve only necessary categories in JSON format through API.

Error Handling

The OpenCart API uses standard HTTP status codes to indicate the success or failure of an API request.

200 OK: The request was successful.
400 Bad Request: The request could not be understood or was missing the required parameters.
401 Unauthorized: Authentication failed or the user does not have permissions for the requested operation.
404 Not Found: The requested resource could not be found.
500 Internal Server Error: An error occurred on the server.

Example Error Response

```
{
 "error": "Invalid API key"
}
```

OpenCart 4 API provides a powerful and flexible way to interact with your OpenCart store programmatically. By leveraging the API, you can integrate various applications, automate processes, and enhance the functionality of your e-commerce platform. This documentation has covered the essential aspects of using the OpenCart API, from authentication and endpoint usage to testing with Postman. Understanding and utilizing these features will empower you to build more efficient, robust, and scalable solutions tailored to your specific business needs. As you continue to explore and implement the OpenCart API, always ensure to follow best practices for security, performance, and maintainability, enabling you to deliver a seamless and enhanced experience for your users.

12. OPENCART MULTI WEBSITES OR STORE SETUP

Opencart multiple websites. It can handle multiple stores with one Opencart installation. Creating a Multi-Store Opencart allows for multi-store management using only one installation. If you have installed Opencart into at least one store, you can add multiple stores to your admin panel without having to repeat the installation process. To add a new store you must first create a subdomain in your cPanel, then add the store in the Settings section of the admin panel.

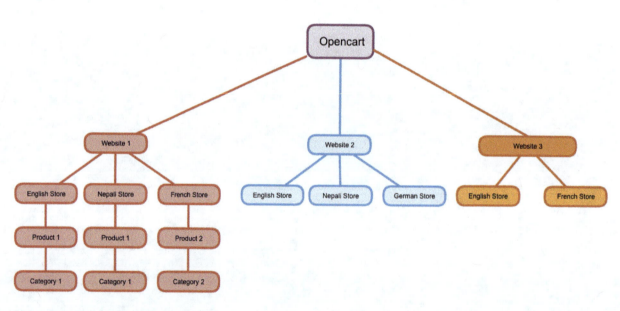

Fig: 12.1

OpenCart 4 allows you to manage multiple online stores from a single admin interface. This multi-site capability is particularly useful for businesses that operate in different regions, sell various product lines, or want to create separate storefronts for different customer segments. Setting up multiple sites in OpenCart is straightforward and provides a centralized way to control and monitor all your stores.

Benefits of a Multisite Setup

- **Centralized Management**: Manage multiple stores from a single admin dashboard. One admin management with one log in for products, categories, customers, orders, design etc

- **Shared Resources**: Use the same product catalog, customer database, and settings across multiple stores. You can configure each product to show on which store and can set different prices for the same product
- **Customized Storefronts**: Tailor the appearance and functionality of each store to target specific audiences. Although having one admin management, you can have different layouts and different themes for different stores
- **Cost-Effective**: Save on infrastructure and maintenance costs by running multiple stores on the same installation.
- **Customer easiness:** Customers can have a single sign-on for different stores that are managed on multiple.

Prerequisites

Before setting up multiple stores, ensure you have the following:

- A working installation of OpenCart 4 on the server (In our example we are using demo.webocreation.com)
- Administrative access to the OpenCart admin panel.
- Domain names or subdomains for each store, both the server and
- DNS Domain name server settings
- You use the addon domain in cpanel to add the 2nd domain to your hosting account. Then change the document root in that 2nd domain to be the same as your first store - the folder opencart is installed in. Add the store to opencart settings and done.
- Point their A records to the IP of your server.
- Associate them with that hosting account which can be done in cPanel via "Aliases" which used to be called "Parked Domains" if I remember correctly.

Example stores

Main store: https://demo.webocreation.com
Store 1: https://demo2.webocreation.com
Store 2: https://demo3.webocreation.com
Store 3: https://dpsignadvertising.com

Step-by-Step Guide to Setting Up Multisite in OpenCart 4
Step 1: Configure Your Domain/Subdomain

First, set up your additional domains or subdomains. This process will vary depending on your hosting provider but generally involves the following steps:

- **DNS management:** Access to domain registrar admin section so you can point domain A records to the server. In this example, we are using Cloudflare DNS so we added the A records like below, as in this example we are using sub-domain demo2.webocreation.com and demo3.webocreation.com, so pointed the A record to the IP address.

Type ▲	Name	Content
A	demo2	91.232.125.3
A	demo3	91.232.125.3
A	🗩 demo	91.232.125.3

Fig: 12.2

For main domains like dpsignadvertising.com, you need to delegate the same name server that you are using for the opencart installed server, here is https://demo.webocreation.com, so for dpsignadvertising.com, we add the same ns1 and ns2 as demo.webocreation.com

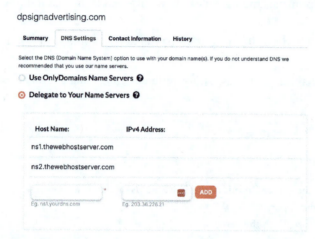

Fig: 12.3

- **Subdomains:** Create subdomains (e.g., store1.yourdomain.com, store2.yourdomain.com) and point them to the OpenCart installation directory.

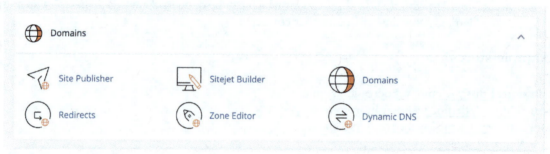

Fig: 12.4

Then click "Create a New Domain" and enter the domain URL and submit, here we entered demo3.webocreation.com

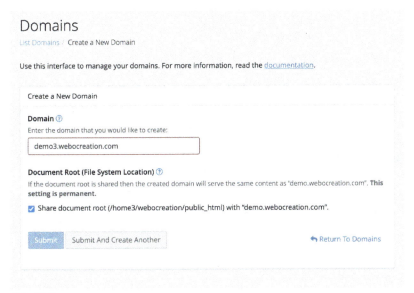

Fig: 12.5

Similarly, you can enter as many domains as needed.

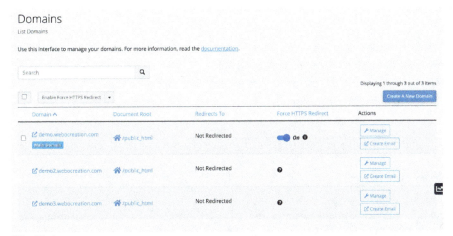

Fig: 12.6

- **Domains:** Same as sub-domains, point each domain to the root directory of your OpenCart installation. We are using the cPanel so we find the domain section, for us here is an example, click in the Domains and enter the domains.

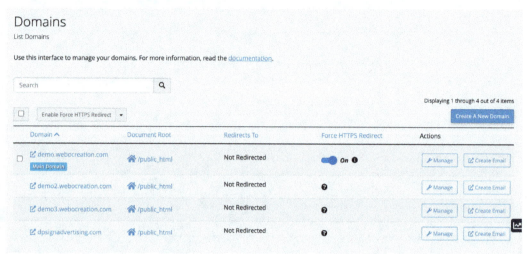

Fig: 12.7

Step 2: Add New Stores in OpenCart Admin

1. **Log in to Admin Panel**: Log in to your OpenCart admin dashboard.
2. **Navigate to Store Settings**: Go to **System -> Settings**.
3. **Add New Store**:
   - Click the "+" button to add a new store.
   - **Store Name**: Enter the name of the new store.
   - **Store URL**: Enter the URL of the new store, including the trailing slashLog in., **https://dpsignadvertising.com/**).

If you forget the trailing slash multi-store will not work

Step 3: Configure Store Settings

1. **General Settings**: Configure general settings such as store name, owner, address, email, and phone number. You can select different themes, logos, and layouts for each store
2. **Local Settings**: Set local settings like country, region, language, and currency for the new store.
3. **Option Settings**: Set all settings like products, legal, etc for the new store.
4. **Image Settings**: Enter the image sizes

Step 4: Customize Your Store

1. **Themes**: Go to **Design -> Themes** and select a theme for your new store. You can choose to use the same theme as your main store or a different one.
2. **Layouts**: Customize the layouts for your new store by navigating to **Design -> Layouts**. Adjust the positions and modules according to your requirements.
3. **Banners and Sliders**: Set up banners and sliders specific to the new store under **Design -> Banners**.

Step 5: Assign Products and Categories

1. **Products**: Navigate to **Catalog -> Products** and edit each product to assign it to the new store. Use the "Stores" tab to select the stores where the product should be visible.
2. **Categories**: Go to **Catalog -> Categories** and assign categories to the new store using the "Stores" tab.

Step 6: Test Your Store

1. **Access the Store URL**: Open a web browser and navigate to the URL of your new store.
2. **Verify Functionality**: Ensure that all links, images, and functionalities are working correctly.
3. **Place a Test Order**: Complete a test purchase to verify that the checkout process is functioning correctly.

Setting up a multisite environment in OpenCart 4 is an efficient way to manage multiple online stores from a single admin interface. By following the steps outlined above, you can configure and customize each store to meet the needs of different markets or customer segments. This powerful feature of OpenCart helps streamline operations, reduce costs, and expand your business reach effectively.

13. OPENCART SEO BEST PRACTICES

Search Engine Optimization (SEO) is essential for enhancing the visibility of your OpenCart store in search engine results. Proper SEO practices can help drive organic traffic, improve user engagement, and increase sales. Here are some best practices to optimize your OpenCart store for search engines.

Admin Setting section changes for the SEO

- Go to Admin >> System >> Settings >> Edit your store
- In the General tab, enter the Meta Title, Meta Tag Description, and Meta Tag Keywords, they are for the Homepage of your store website.
- Go through all of the tabs and enter the contact details, mailing details, server details, etc

SEO-Friendly URLs

SEO-friendly URLs are easier for both search engines and users to read and understand.

- **Enable SEO URLs:** Go to **System -> Settings -> Edit -> Server** and set "Use SEO URLs" to "Yes." If you are using Apache Server then rename the .htaccess.txt to .htaccess. Go to your hosting root folder where Opencart is installed and find .htaccess.txt and rename it to .htaccess
  If you did not find .htaccess.txt then you can paste the following to your .htaccess

  # 1. To use URL Alias you need to be running Apache with mod_rewrite enabled.
  # 2. In your Opencart directory rename htaccess.txt to .htaccess.
  # For any support issues please visit: http://www.Opencart.com
  Options +FollowSymlinks
  # Prevent Directory listing
  Options -Indexes
  # Prevent Direct Access to files
  <FilesMatch "(?i)((\.tpl|.twig|\.ini|\.log|(?<!robots)\.txt))">
  * Require all denied*
  * ## For apache 2.2 and older, replace "Require all denied" with these two lines:*
  * # Order deny, allow*

```
# Deny from all
</FilesMatch>
# SEO URL Settings
RewriteEngine On
# If your Opencart installation does not run on the main web folder make sure you folder it does run in ie. / becomes
/shop/
RewriteBase /
RewriteRule ^sitemap.xml$ index.php?route=extension/feed/google_sitemap [L]
RewriteRule ^googlebase.xml$ index.php?route=extension/feed/google_base [L]
RewriteRule ^system/storage/(.*) index.php?route=error/not_found [L]
RewriteCond %{REQUEST_FILENAME} !-f
RewriteCond %{REQUEST_FILENAME} !-d
RewriteCond %{REQUEST_URI} !.*\.(ico|gif|jpg|jpeg|png|js|css)
RewriteRule ^([^?]*) index.php?_route_=$1 [L,QSA]
### Additional Settings that may need to be enabled for some servers
### Uncomment the commands by removing the # sign in front of it.
### If you get an "Internal Server Error 500" after enabling any of the following settings, restore the # as this
means your host doesn't allow that.
# 1. If your cart only allows you to add one item at a time, it is possible that register_globals is on. This may work to
disable it:
# php_flag register_globals off
# 2. If your cart has magic quotes enabled, This may work to disable it:
# php_flag magic_quotes_gpc Off
# 3. Set max upload file size. Most hosts will limit this and not allow it to be overridden but you can try
# php_value upload_max_filesize 999M
# 4. Set max post size. uncomment this line if you have a lot of product options or are getting errors where forms are
not saving all fields
# php_value post_max_size 999M
# 5. set max time script can take. uncomment this line if you have a lot of product options or are getting errors where
forms are not saving all fields
# php_value max_execution_time 200
# 6. Set max time for input to be received. Uncomment this line if you have a lot of product options or are getting
errors where forms are not saving all fields
# php_value max_input_time 200
# 7. disable open_basedir limitations
# php_admin_value open_basedir none
```

- **Customize URLs**: Use descriptive and keyword-rich URLs. Avoid using default or numeric IDs in URLs.
- Remove index.php?route= in Opencart for contact, home, and other

Optimize Product and Category Pages

Product name and Description – Content is the key for Search Engines
– Product description, as best practices for SEO, you should aim to write at least 300 words but be clear and write as much as possible.

– Name the images as the product name, in Opencart most of the image's alt tags are either product name in the product page, category name in category image, and so on.

Titles and Meta Descriptions

- **Unique Titles**: Ensure each product and category page has a unique and descriptive title. Include relevant keywords naturally.
- **Meta Descriptions**: Write unique and compelling meta descriptions for each page. Use primary keywords and make them enticing to encourage clicks.

Headings and Content

- **Use Headings**: Properly structure your content using **<h1>**, **<h2>**, and other heading tags. The main product or category name should be in an **<h1>** tag.
- **Quality Content**: Write detailed and informative descriptions for products and categories. Include keywords naturally and focus on providing value to the reader.
- **Enter SEO information for Products, Categories, Information pages, and Manufacturers.**
  To enter the Products SEO information, go to Admin >> Catalog >> Products >> Add/Edit >> Then in the General tab, enter the Meta Tag Title, Meta Tag Description, and Meta Tag Keywords, likewise go to the SEO tab and enter the keyword for each store.
  While entering the Meta Tag title, consider the following best practices:
  – Google only shows around 50–60 characters of a title tag so make the title tag around 50-60 characters
  – Put important keywords in the title and meta description
  While entering the Meta Tag Description, consider the following best practices:
  – 160 characters long
  – We have seen search engines always do not pick the meta description but enter them.
  – Better not to include double quotation marks
  While entering the SEO keyword:
  – Include the main keyword or product name and better to use lowercase and not to use prepositions words
  – Better not to use underscore (_), instead use dashes (-)
  – Better not to include double quotation marks or single quotation and special characters

  Follow same for Admin >> Catalog >> Categories and Admin >> Catalog >> Information and Admin >> Catalog >> Manufacturers

Image Optimization

Images play a crucial role in an e-commerce store but can impact your SEO if not optimized correctly.

- **Alt Text**: Use descriptive alt text for images. This helps search engines understand the content of the images and improves accessibility.
- **File Names**: Use keyword-rich file names for images instead of generic names like **IMG001.jpg**.
- **Image Compression**: Compress images to reduce load times without compromising quality. Faster loading pages improve user experience and SEO.

Internal Linking

Internal links help search engines understand the structure of your site and the relationship between different pages.

- **Link to Related Products**: On product pages, link to related or complementary products.
- **Breadcrumbs**: Use breadcrumb navigation to help users and search engines navigate your site more easily.

Mobile Optimization

With the increasing number of mobile users, it's crucial to ensure your OpenCart store is mobile-friendly.

- **Responsive Design**: Use a responsive theme that adjusts to different screen sizes and devices.
- **Mobile Speed**: Optimize your site for fast loading on mobile devices. Use tools like Google's PageSpeed Insights to identify and fix issues.

Enable the sitemap extension

Find sitemap extensions and install them, one for Opencart 4 is https://webocreation.com/google-sitemap-opencart-4-module-or-extension-for-free/
G to Admin >> Extensions >> Extensions >> Choose the extension type >> Feeds then install the Google Sitemap extension and then edit it and change the status to "Enabled" and save it. Now your sitemap URL will be given there which looks like this:
https://yourwebsiteurl.com/index.php?route=extension/feed/google_sitemap

Create a Google Webmasters account and Bing Webmaster account and submit the above sitemap URL in them.

Add robots.txt

Create robots.txt in the root folder where Opencart is installed, and in that robots.txt place the following text, here change the sitemap URL to your website URL

*User-agent: ***
Disallow: /admin
Sitemap: https://yourwebsiteurl.com/index.php?route=extension/feed/google_sitemap

Canonical URL

Opencart supports canonical URL automatically, be sure to check it, it removes the duplicate content penalties. https://yourwebsiteurl.com/cateogryname/productname and https://yourwebsiteurl.com/productname, these both URLs point to the same product page, so Google may take it as duplicate content so canonical URLs need to be set up. One example is when you view the source of the code you will see the canonical URL something like the below:

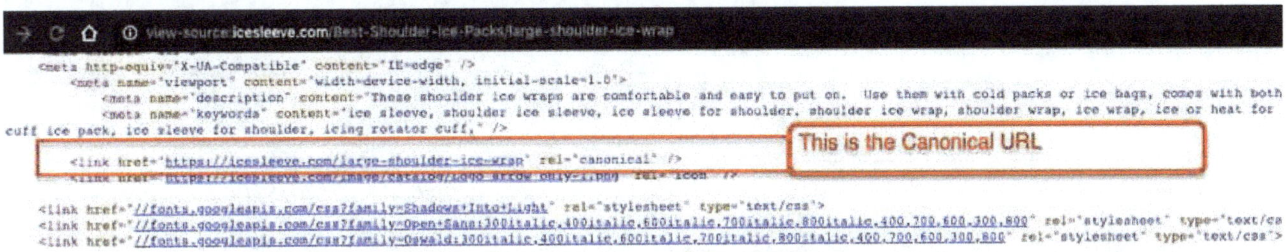

Fig: 13.1

127

Social proof

Use social proof to gain user trust and keep your visitors engaged in your website
Link to your website on all social media profiles. Social proof is for customers' confidence. The footer has options to keep the user engaged (social media, phone number, etc)

Schema Markup

Schema markup helps search engines understand the content of your pages and can improve the visibility of your listings in SERPs.

- **Product Schema**: Use schema markup for product pages to provide search engines with detailed product information, such as price, availability, and reviews.
- **Breadcrumb Schema**: Implement breadcrumb schema to enhance how your site is displayed in search results.

Site Speed and Performance

Site speed is a significant factor in SEO. Faster sites provide a better user experience and are favored by search engines. Use the right cache module to get more benefits we missed Litespeed plugins in our WordPress website which site was slow, so better to ask your hosting server which caches are supported. Check with the Google page speed and follow their suggestions to improve the page speed. Improving the Google PageSpeed insights score will help a lot to show in the search results.

- **Caching**: Use caching to reduce server load and speed up page loading times.
- **Optimize Code**: Minify CSS, JavaScript, and HTML to reduce file sizes and improve load times.
- **Content Delivery Network (CDN)**: Use a CDN to serve your content faster to users across different geographical locations.

Srcset for images

Use srcset for images which helps properly size the images as per the screen Load images properly as per the screen with srcset you can load different images for different screens. one example image code:

```
▼<div class="wp-block-image">
  ▼<figure class="aligncenter">
    <img data-lazyloaded="1" src="https://i1.wp.com/webocreation.com/blog/wp-content/uploads/2019/08/out-of-stock-admin-
    setting.jpg?w=696&ssl=1" alt="Out of Stock Admin Settings" class="wp-image-6378 litespeed-loaded" data-sizes="(max-
    width: 696px) 100vw, 696px" width="1" height="1" scale="0" sizes="(max-width: 696px) 100vw, 696px" srcset="https://
    i1.wp.com/webocreation.com/blog/wp-content/uploads/2019/08/out-of-stock-admin-setting.jpg?w=800&ssl=1 800w, https://
    i1.wp.com/webocreation.com/blog/wp-content/uploads/2019/08/out-of-stock-admin-setting.jpg?resize=300%2C229&ssl=1 300w,
    https://i1.wp.com/webocreation.com/blog/wp-content/uploads/2019/08/out-of-stock-admin-setting.jpg?
    resize=768%2C586&ssl=1 768w, https://i1.wp.com/webocreation.com/blog/wp-content/uploads/2019/08/out-of-stock-admin-
    setting.jpg?resize=80%2C60&ssl=1 80w, https://i1.wp.com/webocreation.com/blog/wp-content/uploads/2019/08/out-of-stock-
    admin-setting.jpg?resize=696%2C531&ssl=1 696w, https://i1.wp.com/webocreation.com/blog/wp-content/uploads/2019/08/out-
    of-stock-admin-setting.jpg?resize=551%2C420&ssl=1 551w" data-was-processed="true"> == $0
    ▶ <noscript>…</noscript>
  </figure>
</div>
```

Fig: 13.2

See the code *srcset="https://i1.wp.com/webocreation.com/wp-content/uploads/2019/08/out-of-stock-admin-setting.jpg?w=800&ssl=1 800w, https://i1.wp.com/webocreation.com/wp-content/uploads/2019/08/out-of-stock-admin-setting.jpg?resize=300%2C229&ssl=1 300w, https://i1.wp.com/webocreation.com/wp-content/uploads/2019/08/out-of-stock-admin-setting.jpg?resize=768%2C586&ssl=1 768w, https://i1.wp.com/webocreation.com/wp-content/uploads/2019/08/out-of-stock-admin-setting.jpg?resize=80%2C60&ssl=1 80w, https://i1.wp.com/webocreation.com/wp-content/uploads/2019/08/out-of-stock-admin-*

setting.jpg?resize=696%2C531&ssl=1 696w, https://i1.wp.com/webocreation.com/wp-content/uploads/2019/08/out-of-stock-admin-setting.jpg?resize=551%2C420&ssl=1 551w" this loads the images as per the width of the screen. We didn't find any module for this, we will try to provide it soon, so for now, developer help is needed.

https://developers.google.com/web/tools/lighthouse/audits/oversized-images

GZIP Compression

GZIP for more efficient transfer to requesting clients. The compression level must be between 0 – 9. To enable the text compression in Opencart, go to Admin >> System >> Settings >> Server tab >> Add the "Output Compression Level". The value should be 0-9, what we find out is most of the time it works above 5 but hit and trial is the only option that we see. With these, it minimizes the byte size of network responses and fewer bytes means the page loads fast.

Webfont loading

Developer or Designer tasks: Ensure text remains visible during Webfont load
 Follow the idea provided at https://developers.google.com/web/updates/2016/02/font-display. Just for your information, we tried that and in our case, we used *font-display: swap,* and only works. Something like below:
@font-face {
font-family: 'Arvo';
font-display: swap;
 src: local('Arvo'), url(https://fonts.gstatic.com/s/arvo/v9/rC7kKhY-eUDY-ucISTIf5PesZW2xOQ-xsNqO47m55DA.woff2) format('woff2');
 }

Fix broken links

Broken links on the website are harmful to SEO. So one freeway to check the broken link is https://www.brokenlinkcheck.com/

Fig: 13.3
Once it finds the broken links then fix them or remove them.

Add your Business to Google

Open https://business.google.com and add your business details.

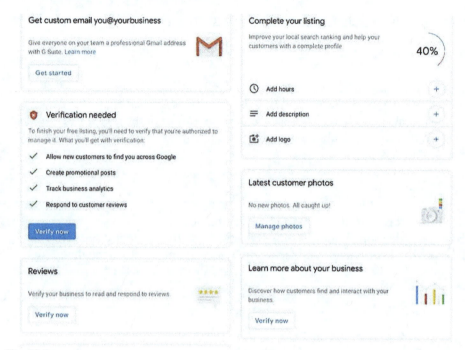

Fig: 13.4

Best practices for SEO as they relate to local searches include creating a Google My Business page. This practice is especially important for brick-and-mortar businesses as it shows a rich result on local Google SERPs.

301 Redirects

There are no functionalities by default to do 301 redirects but you can use free extensions from the Opencart marketplace and you can redirect old URLs to new URLs, if you have to change the SEO URL keyword then don't forget to add the 301 redirects.

SSL certificates

Add an SSL certificate to your site and redirect to the same host. For safety, security, and customer confidence. All domains are to be redirected to the same host as https://yourwebsiteurl.com, choose www or non-www redirect to one, and use one.

Mobile-first approach

Mobile-first approach and Use a responsive, mobile-friendly design. Mobile-friendly is for mobile fitness, as Google search started to index the mobile-first, so be sure you don't hide things on a mobile phone and show them on a desktop, if it is hidden on the mobile then Google search will no see it, we found is it checks for the content, links count to see if it is similar with the desktop view and mobile view.

Regular Monitoring and Analysis

SEO is an ongoing process. Regularly monitor your site's performance and make necessary adjustments.

- **Analytics Tools**: Use tools like Google Analytics and Google Search Console to track your SEO performance.
- **Keyword Analysis**: Regularly perform keyword research to identify new opportunities and trends.
- **SEO Audits**: Conduct periodic SEO audits to identify and fix issues.

Implementing these SEO best practices can significantly improve the visibility and performance of your OpenCart store in search engine results. By focusing on optimizing product and category pages, using SEO-friendly URLs, optimizing images, improving internal linking, ensuring mobile optimization, using schema markup, enhancing site speed, and regularly monitoring your site's performance, you can drive more traffic, enhance user experience, and ultimately increase sales. Stay proactive and keep up with the latest SEO trends to maintain and improve your search engine rankings.

14. OPENCART SPEED OPTIMIZATION

In this Opencart tutorial on website speed optimization, we are showing you 10 ways to speed up the Opencart 4 which you can do from the free Opencart module and tips provided below. This helps to optimize website speed in Opencart and increase Opencart load speed.

Choose a better hosting provider and better cache module

Just choose a <u>better hosting provider of Opencart</u>, better is always expensive so choose as per your budget. Choose a good cache module for Opencart. If you are using the shared hosting then ask them which cache they are providing and use the cache module as per it, our is using LSCache so we use the LSCache module.

<u>Download the page speed Opencart module</u>

Defer all the extra CSS and JS at the footer.

In the module, we just defer all the JavaScript with '*defer="defer"*', with this, the script will not run until after the page has loaded, better to use only for the external scripts.

```
<script defer='defer' src="catalog/view/javascript/bootstrap/js/bootstrap.min.js"
type="text/javascript"></script>
```

```
<script src="catalog/view/javascript/common.js" type="text/javascript"></script>
```

For jQuery, we load at first because it is a building block so we load at header and without defer. The following is the Ocmod XML that makes those changes.

```
<file path="catalog/controller/common/header.php">
  <operation>
    <search>
     <![CDATA[
        $data['links'] = $this->document->getLinks();
     ]]>
    </search>
```

```xml
  <add position="replace">
    <![CDATA[
      $data['links'] ="";
        //$data['links'] = $this->document->getLinks();
      ]]>
  </add>
 </operation>
 <operation>
  <search><![CDATA[
  $data['styles'] = $this->document->getStyles();
]]>   </search>
   <add position="replace"><![CDATA[
    $data['styles'] ="";
 //$data['styles'] = $this->document->getStyles();
]]>   </add>
 </operation>
</file>
<file path="catalog/controller/common/footer.php">
 <operation>
   <search><![CDATA[
  $data['scripts'] = $this->document->getScripts('footer');
]]>   </search>
   <add position="after"><![CDATA[
  $data['links'] = $this->document->getLinks();
  $data['styles'] = $this->document->getStyles();
   //$data['scripts'] = $this->document->getScripts();
]]>   </add>
  </operation>
</file>
<file path="catalog/view/theme/*/template/common/header.twig">
  <operation>
   <search><![CDATA[
<script src="catalog/view/javascript/bootstrap/js/bootstrap.min.js" type="text/javascript"></script>
]]>   </search>
   <add position="replace" offset="6"><![CDATA[
<!--<script src="catalog/view/javascript/bootstrap/js/bootstrap.min.js" type="text/javascript"></script>
<link href="catalog/view/javascript/font-awesome/css/font-awesome.min.css" rel="stylesheet" type="text/css" />
<link href="//fonts.googleapis.com/css?family=Open+Sans:400,400i,300,700" rel="stylesheet" type="text/css" />
<link href="catalog/view/theme/default/stylesheet/stylesheet.css" rel="stylesheet">-->
]]>   </add>
  </operation>
  <operation>
   <search><![CDATA[
<script src="catalog/view/javascript/common.js" type="text/javascript"></script>
]]>   </search>
```

```
<add position="replace" offset="3"><![CDATA[
<!--<script src="catalog/view/javascript/common.js" type="text/javascript"></script>-->
]]>  </add>
  </operation>
</file>
<file path="catalog/view/theme/*/template/common/footer.twig">
  <operation>
    <search>
      <![CDATA[{% for script in scripts %}]]>
    </search>
    <add position="before"><![CDATA[
<link href="catalog/view/javascript/bootstrap/css/bootstrap.min.css" rel="stylesheet" media="screen" />
<link href="catalog/view/javascript/font-awesome/css/fonPhotoshop.min.css" rel="stylesheet" type="text/css" />
<link href="//fonts.googleapis.com/css?family=Open+Sans:400,400i,300,700" rel="stylesheet" type="text/css" />
<link href="catalog/view/theme/default/stylesheet/stylesheet.css" rel="stylesheet">
{% for style in styles %}
<link href="{{ style.href }}" type="text/css" rel="{{ style.rel }}" media="{{ style.media }}" />
{% endfor %}
{% for link in links %}
<link href="{{ link.href }}" rel="{{ link.rel }}" />
{% endfor %}
<script defer="defer" src="catalog/view/javascript/bootstrap/js/bootstrap.min.js" type="text/javascript"></script>
<script src="catalog/view/javascript/common.js" type="text/javascript"></script>
]]>  </add>
  </operation>
</file>
```

Use the image sizes properly

One idea to size the image is to use the ration in all image settings. The best image ratio is 16:9. So, create images of size 1200px width and 675 px height and in all settings use a 16:9 ratio. Go to Admin >> Extensions >> Extensions >> Choose Theme as extension type >> Then edit your active theme >> Then enter the sizes for Images in the ratio of 16:9, like we are using it as:

Fig: 14.1

Use the proper extension for the image:

JPEGs are for photographs and realistic images. PNGs are for line art, text-heavy images, and images with few colors. See the difference

PNG used, loading time is 1.56 and page size is 824.5   JPEG uploaded, load time is just 413ms and page size 72.3kb

Fig: 14.2

You can easily convert the PNG to JPG or JPG to PNG online as well as in Photoshop. Like:

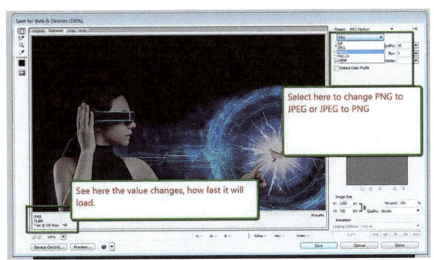

Fig: 14.3

Optimize the image properly

Use the ImageOptim for properly optimizing the image. It optimizes as per the page speed insight. You can download the ImageOptim here. Right-click the image and open with ImageOptim and it will optimize and replace the image with an optimized one.

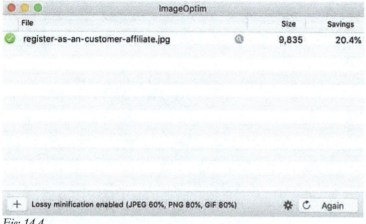

Fig: 14.4

Lazy loading of images:

Just adding loading=”lazy” in the image tag will lazy load the images.

<img loading="lazy" src="catalog/language/en-gb/en-gb.png" alt="English" title="English">

Created one module for lazy loading of the image:

```
<file path="catalog/view/theme/*/*/*/*.twig\catalog/view/theme/*/template/*/*/*.twig">
 <operation>
  <search>
   <![CDATA[<img ]]>
  </search>
  <add position="replace">
   <![CDATA[<img loading="lazy"  ]]>
  </add>
 </operation>
</file>
```

GZIP compression level

Gzip Compression is an effective way to reduce the size of files. To enable the text compression in Opencart, go to Admin >> System >> Settings >> Server tab >> Add the "Output Compression Level". The value should be 0-9, what we find out is most of the time it works above 5 but hit and trial is the only option that we see. With these, it minimizes the byte size of network responses and fewer bytes means the page loads fast.

Speed up the repeat visit by serving static assets with an efficient cache policy

You can serve static assets with an efficient cache policy by adding the following code in the .htaccess file, these are just our ideas, you can make changes as per your requirement:

```
# Set up 1 week caching on javascript and CSS
<FilesMatch "\.(js|css)$">
ExpiresDefault A604800
Header append Cache-Control "proxy-revalidate"
SetOutputFilter DEFLATE
</FilesMatch>
# LBROWSERCSTART Browser Caching
<IfModule mod_expires.c>
ExpiresActive On
ExpiresByType image/gif "access 1 year"
ExpiresByType image/jpg "access 1 year"
ExpiresByType image/jpeg "access 1 year"
ExpiresByType image/png "access 1-year"
ExpiresByType image/x-icon "access 1 year"
ExpiresByType text/css "access 1 month"
ExpiresByType text/javascript "access 1 month"
ExpiresByType text/html "access 1 month"
ExpiresByType application/javascript "access 1-month"
ExpiresByType application/x-javascript "access 1 month"
ExpiresByType application/xhtml-xml "access 1 month"
ExpiresByType application/pdf "access 1 month"
ExpiresByType application/x-shockwave-flash "access 1 month"
ExpiresDefault "access 1 month"
</IfModule>
# END Caching LBROWSERCEND
```

Compress and minify the o1-year

```
<file path="system/library/response.php">
 <operation>
  <search position="replace"><![CDATA[
   public function output() {
 ]]>
  </search>
  <add><![CDATA[
   public function output() {
    if ($this->output) {
       $this->output = preg_replace("/(\n)+/", "\n", $this->output);
       $this->output = preg_replace("/\r\n+/", "\n", $this->output);
       $this->output = preg_replace("/\n(\t)+/", "\n", $this->output);
       $this->output = preg_replace("/\n(\ )+/", "\n", $this->output);
       $this->output = preg_replace("/\>(\n)+</", '><', $this->output);
       $this->output = preg_replace("/\>\r\n</", '><', $this->output);
    }
  ]]><
  </add>
```

```
</operation>
</file>
```

Minify your HTML, CSS, and JS

```
<file path="system/library/template.php">
 <operation>
  <search><![CDATA[return $this->adaptor->render($template, $cache);]]></search>
  <add position="replace"><![CDATA[
if (strpos($template, 'template/') !== false) {
    return $this->minify($this->adaptor->render($template, $cache));
} else {
    return $this->adaptor->render($template, $cache);
}
    ]]>    </add>
</operation>
<operation>
  <search><![CDATA[private $adaptor;]]></search>
  <add position="after"><![CDATA[
  /**
   * @param  string  $body
   * @return string
   */
  public function minify($body) {
      $search = array(
          '/\>[^\S ]+/s',    // strip whitespaces after tags, except space
          '/[^\S ]+\</s',    // strip whitespaces before tags, except space
          '/(\s)+/s',        // shorten multiple whitespace sequences
      );
      $replace = array(
          '>',
          '<',
          '\\1',
          ''
      );
      $body = preg_replace($search, $replace, $body);
      return $body;
  }
 ]]>
  </add>
 </operation>
</file>
```

Index the database table

First backup your database. Confirm your back works. Backup again.
Download the turbo.php, upload it where Opencart is installed, run YOURSITEURL/turbo.php, and click the "Add Database Indexes' button, this will index all the database tables as per column name.

https://github.com/lilalaunesau/Opencart-turbo/blob/master/turbo.php

Or you can run following SQL directly in your database:

```
ALTER TABLE `oc_category` ADD INDEX ( `parent_id` ) ;
ALTER TABLE `oc_category` ADD INDEX ( `top` ) ;
ALTER TABLE `oc_category` ADD INDEX ( `sort_order` ) ;
ALTER TABLE `oc_category` ADD INDEX ( `status` ) ;
ALTER TABLE `oc_category_description` ADD INDEX ( `language_id` );
ALTER TABLE `oc_category_to_store` ADD INDEX ( `store_id` );
ALTER TABLE `oc_category_path` ADD INDEX ( `path_id` );
ALTER TABLE `oc_product` ADD INDEX ( `model` ) ;
ALTER TABLE `oc_product` ADD INDEX ( `sku` ) ;
ALTER TABLE `oc_product` ADD INDEX ( `upc` ) ;
ALTER TABLE `oc_product` ADD INDEX ( `manufacturer_id` ) ;
ALTER TABLE `oc_product` ADD INDEX ( `sort_order` ) ;
ALTER TABLE `oc_product` ADD INDEX ( `status` ) ;
ALTER TABLE `oc_product_option` ADD INDEX ( `option_id` ) ;
ALTER TABLE `oc_product_option_value` ADD INDEX ( `product_option_id` ) ;
ALTER TABLE `oc_product_option_value` ADD INDEX ( `product_id` ) ;
ALTER TABLE `oc_product_option_value` ADD INDEX ( `option_id` ) ;
ALTER TABLE `oc_product_option_value` ADD INDEX ( `option_value_id` ) ;
ALTER TABLE `oc_product_to_category` ADD INDEX ( `category_id` );
ALTER TABLE `oc_product_attribute` ADD INDEX ( `attribute_id` );
ALTER TABLE `oc_product_attribute` ADD INDEX ( `language_id` );
ALTER TABLE `oc_product_description` ADD INDEX ( `language_id` );
ALTER TABLE `oc_product_to_store` ADD INDEX ( `store_id` );
ALTER TABLE `oc_option` ADD INDEX ( `sort_order` ) ;
ALTER TABLE `oc_option_description` ADD INDEX ( `name` ) ;
ALTER TABLE `oc_option_value` ADD INDEX ( `option_id` ) ;
ALTER TABLE `oc_option_value_description` ADD INDEX ( `option_id` ) ;
ALTER TABLE `oc_url_alias` ADD INDEX ( `query` ) ;
ALTER TABLE `oc_url_alias` ADD INDEX ( `keyword` ) ;
ALTER TABLE `oc_url_alias` ADD INDEX ( `url_alias_id` );
```

Developer or Designer tasks: Ensure text remains visible during Webfont load

Follow the idea provided at https://developers.google.com/web/updates/2016/02/font-display. Just for your information, we tried that and in our case, we used *font-display: swap*, and it only works. Something like below:

```
@font-face {
    font-family: 'Arvo';
    font-display: swap;
    src: local('Arvo'), url(https://fonts.gstatic.com/s/arvo/v9/rC7kKhY-eUDY-ucISTIf5PesZW2xOQ-xsNqO47m55DA.woff2)
format('woff2');
}
```

Look for Critical CSS: Defer unused CSS, remove all unused CSS on a page, and try to target CSS for each page.

https://developers.google.com/web/tools/lighthouse/audits/unused-css

Caching

```
$country_data = $this->cache->get('country. admin');
if (!$country_data) {
        $query = $this->db->query("SELECT * FROM `" . DB_PREFIX . "country` ORDER BY `name` ASC");
        $country_data = $query->rows;
        $this->cache->set('country. admin', $country_data);
}
```

CDN - setup Cloudflare easily for eCommerce websites

In this tutorial, we set up Cloudflare CDN for eCommerce websites like Opencart, three steps are: first create a Cloudflare account, add a website domain in the Cloudflare dashboard, and change the DNS records of your domain. We show you how to fix the SSL issues that we face in Cloudflare, how to connect FTP after Cloudflare is set up, and finally how to log the real visitors' IP than the Cloudflare IP.

Let's take an example of https://dpsignadvertising.com where we install Opencart, register this domain at onlydomains.com, and delegate to name servers:

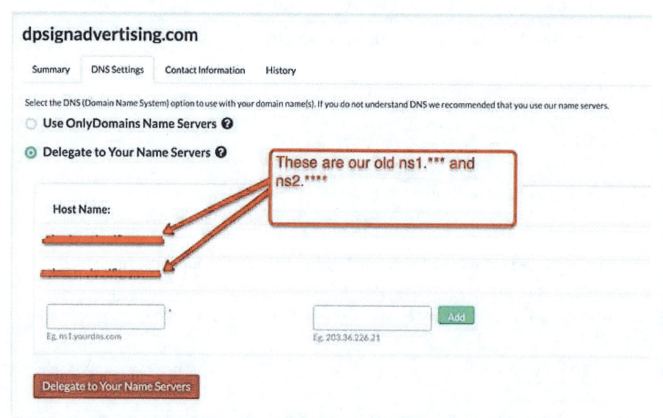

Fig: 14.5

It is similar in your DNS settings also, mostly we point to servers ns1 and ns2.

Let's create a Cloudflare account

- Go to https://dash.cloudflare.com/sign-up.
- Enter your email and password.

- Click Create Account.
- You will get an email like below

Now it's time to add a domain to Cloudflare. If you follow the steps while registering an account then it will directly take you to add the site.

- Log in to your Cloudflare account.
- Click on **Add Site** from the top navigation bar.

Accelerate and protect your site with Cloudflare

Enter your site (example.com):

Add site

Want to add multiple sites? Learn how.

Fig: 14.6

- Enter your website URL and then click "Add Site".
- Then you need to select the plan as per your need, we are using a free plan, select the free plan and click "Confirm plan"
- Now Cloudflare attempts to automatically identify your DNS records and shows lists of DNS results, for dpsignadvertising.com it is showing as in the image:

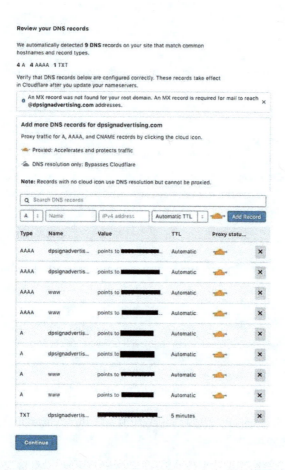

Fig: 14.7

Be careful and check for missing DNS records, mostly MX records if you have setup. Then, click **Continue**.

- Now you will see like NS records of Cloudflare:
- Now login to the domain registrar, in our case is onlydomains.com and we changed the NS1 and NS2, now it looks like in the image below:

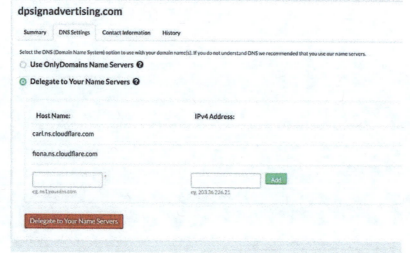

Fig: 14.8

- Once you click "Delegate to your Name Servers", sometimes it takes up to 24hrs to 48 hours, in our case, it was done within 10 mins and we received an email like the one below:

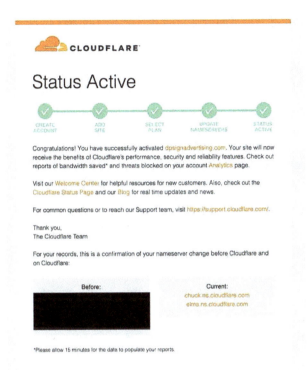

Fig: 14.9

- Once you got an email your Cloudflare is active and you can see the active status in the Cloudflare admin. Similarly, you can see the analytics that it is serving.

Fig: 14.10

How to solve the SSL issue of Cloudflare?

Go to Cloudflare Dashboard >> Click SSL/TLS >> Edge Certificates >> Then toggle to ON for "Always Use HTTPS"

Fig: 14.11

Then the SSL issues are resolved.

Cloudflare FTP issues: The solution to FTP Cloudflare issues: With Cloudflare set up, you will not be able to connect to your FTP with the domain name so you need to use the IP of your server. You can find the Cloudflare Dashboard >> DNS >> Then find the FTP IP or your website URL IP. Or set up ftp url and off the proxy for the FTP URL

Fig: 14.12

Get the actual visitors' IP address rather than the Cloudflare IP address in Opencart. If you are using Google Analytics then you may see the same Cloudflare IP address as the visitor's IP address as all IPs are proxied by Cloudflare. Sometimes, the Payment gateway may block all the payments as well and it will see the same IP ordering the products which may create suspicious activities, so to fix that you need to add the following code at the top of **index.php**

```
if (isset($_SERVER["HTTP_CF_CONNECTING_IP"])) {
  $_SERVER['REMOTE_ADDR'] = $_SERVER["HTTP_CF_CONNECTING_IP"];
}
```

Cloudflare can be used on any website so it does not stick to Opencart, with the above you can enable Cloudflare on any website.

Speed optimization is a continuous process that requires regular monitoring and adjustments. By implementing the practices outlined above—optimizing images, using caching, minifying files, leveraging a CDN, optimizing your database, choosing a reliable hosting provider, enabling Gzip compression, reducing HTTP requests, leveraging browser caching, and optimizing the OpenCart codebase—you can significantly enhance the performance of your OpenCart store. A faster website not only improves the user experience but also boosts SEO rankings, ultimately leading to higher conversions and sales.

15. OPENCART SECURITY MEASURES

In this Opencart tips and tricks, we are showing you 25 Opencart security tactics to make Opencart's website secure by providing a cheat sheet for Opencart eCommerce users, so that the customers can buy products confidently which may increase your conversion rates. Here are the 25 lists of things that you can do to make the Opencart website secure:

Use good and secure hosting

Research and buy good, reliable, and secure hosting.

Check if the install/ folder is still there

Once Opencart is installed, you need to remove or delete the install/ folder. Renaming the folder will also have a security hole. Thus, always delete the install/ folder.

Proper Security settings in the admin

Login to the admin section >> System >> Settings >> Edit required store >> Then in the Server tab, select the use SSL to Yes

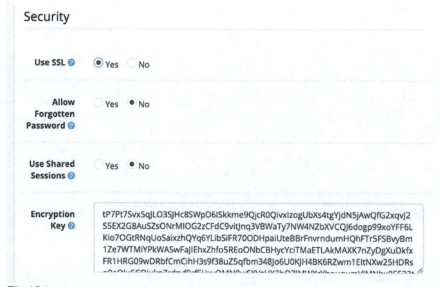

Fig: 15.1

Use SSL: To use SSL check with your host if an SSL certificate is installed and add the SSL URL to the catalog and admin config files.

Allow Forgotten Password: Allow forgotten passwords to be used for the admin. This will be disabled automatically if the system detects a hack attempt.

Use Shared Sessions: Try to share the session cookie between stores so the cart can be passed between different domains.

Encryption Key: Please provide a secret key that will be used to encrypt private information when processing orders.

Use HTTPS/SSL Certificate

Selecting SSL to Yes on the above setting will not give you an HTTPS URL, your server also needs to have SSL installed. Nowadays most servers provide free encrypt SSL certificates which can be set up with just some clicks, or you can use more secure SSL certificates.

One thing you need to take care of is all of your URL links need to start with HTTPS:// instead of HTTP:// else it will not be fully secured. If you are using external URLs, make sure they start with HTTPS://. With proper SSL installation, your URL will look like the below when you click on the SSL icon:

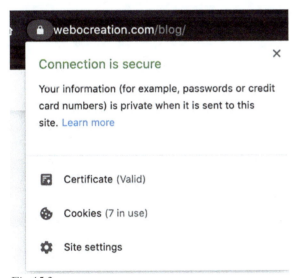

Fig: 15.2

Protect your storage/ folder and other files like the *config.php* file and admin/config.php

Keep storage/ folder outside of the public_html folder. In the image below, our storage folder is v3storage. Similarly, check your file permission and keep it below 0644.

Fig: 15.3

Use the latest PHP version

See the chart PHP V5.6 is already at the end of its life which means there will be no update of security, and they are exposed to unpatched security vulnerabilities. So for security always use the latest version of PHP. Likewise, performance also increased in the latest version of PHP 8 as well which had a good impact.

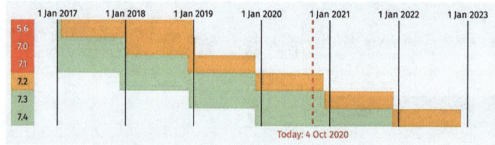

Fig: 15.4: https://www.php.net/supported-versions.php

Use Anti-fraud extension

Opencart by default provides some Anti-fraud extensions, that help store owner secure their online e-commerce website from malicious fraudsters and make them more secure. Login to admin >> Extensions >> Extensions >> Choose the extension type as Anti-Fraud >> Then you will see lists of modules that you can use. You can use some of them for free like 500 queries/month.

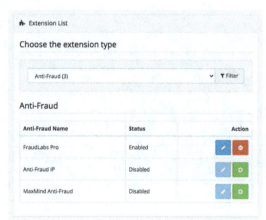

Fig: 15.5

Error handling setting

Enable error logging into the error.log file and it will insert into the database. It is a better idea not to display errors. If you display errors then it will show all full paths of files and it may help hackers. While you perform your debugging errors you can enable it but for security reasons keep it checked as No. You can set the error handling at admin >> System >> Settings >> edit Your Store >> Server tab and you will see the error handling section at the end.

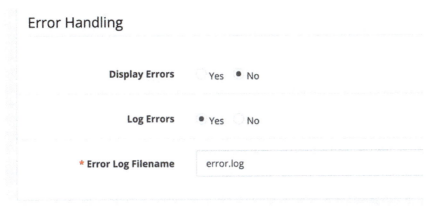

Fig: 15.6

Monitor your admin error logs

Analyzing error logs also shows what issues are happening and fixing them is important. Similarly, check logs at admin >> Extensions >> Modifications >> Log tab. Fixing errors makes the site more secure.

Block bad bots

Opencart provides settings for Robots. You can get it at admin >> System >> Settings >> Edit Your Store >> Server tab and you can see the Robots field. A list of web crawler user agents that shared sessions will not be used with. Use separate lines for each user agent.

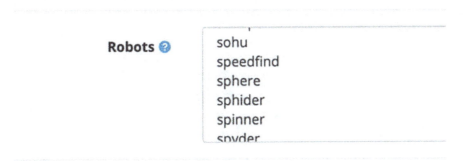

Fig: 15.7

You can set it in the .htaccess file like below as well, if you are using Nginx then you need to write code that returns 403 or so.

RewriteCond %{HTTP_USER_AGENT} ^.(agent1 | Wget | Catall Spider).*$ [NC]*
RewriteRule . - [F,L]*

Allowed File extensions and allowed file mime type permissions

Opencart by default has options to restrict file extensions and file mime types.

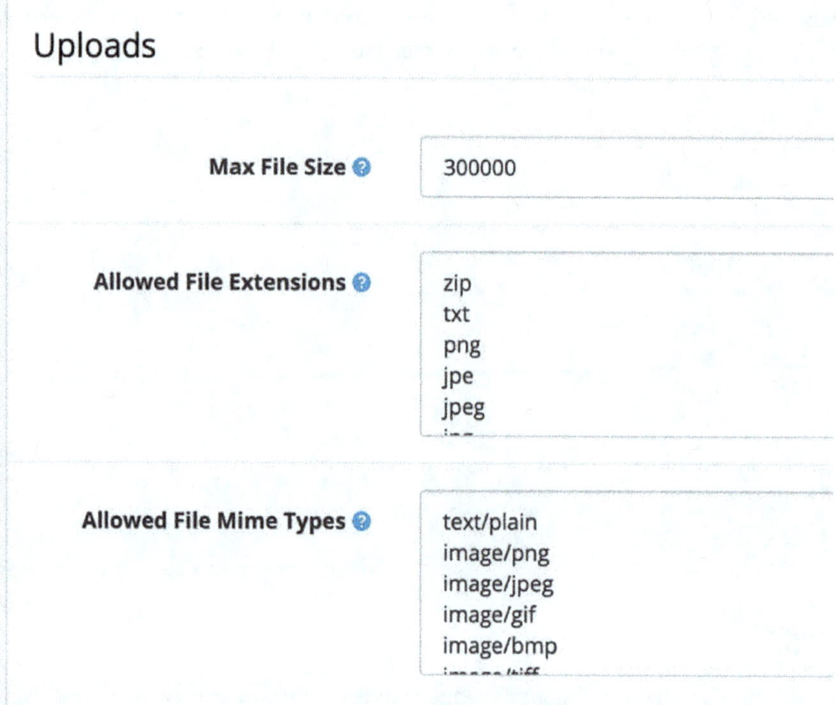

Uploads

Max File Size ❓	300000
Allowed File Extensions ❓	zip txt png jpe jpeg
Allowed File Mime Types ❓	text/plain image/png image/jpeg image/gif image/bmp

Fig: 15.8

Allowed File Extensions: Add which file extensions are allowed to be uploaded. Use a new line for each value.

zip

txt

png

jpe

jpeg

jpg

gif

bmp

ico

tiff

tif

svg

svgz

zip

rar

msi

cab

mp3

qt

mov
pdf
psd
ai
eps
ps
doc

Allowed File Mime type: Add which file mime types are allowed to be uploaded. Use a new line for each value.

text/plain
image/png
image/jpeg
image/gif
image/bmp
image/tiff
image/svg+xml
application/zip
"application/zip"
application/x-zip
"application/x-zip"
application/x-zip-compressed
"application/x-zip-compressed"
application/rar
"application/rar"
application/x-rar
"application/x-rar"
application/x-rar-compressed
"application/x-rar-compressed"
application/octet-stream
"application/octet-stream"
audio/mpeg
video/quicktime
application/pdf

Be sure there are no PHP and JS. In this way, you can secure your file upload buttons.

Review All Users, User Groups, and Grant the Minimum Permissions Necessary

Go to admin >> System >> Users and see all users and verify what user group is assigned. Then check all User groups and see what access permission and modification permissions are given. Try to grant the minimum permissions as necessary. In Opencart you can make as many User groups as you want.

Use a strong username and password

Set a strong password. Better not to use admin as a username.

Opencart V4 has Max Login Attempts. Maximum login attempts are allowed before the account is locked for 1 hour. Customer and affiliate accounts can be unlocked on the customer or affiliate admin pages.

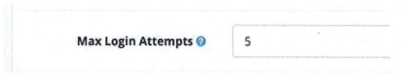

Fig: 15.9

It is available only on Opencart v3 but you can implement this by following the tutorials at https://forum.Opencart.com/viewtopic.php?t=218405#p790296

Two-factor Authentication free module

You can use two-factor authentication but need to use extensions that are available in the Opencart marketplace

API security in Opencart

Similarly, check your API access as well. Go to admin >> System >> Users >> API and review all your API usernames and set proper API usernames, API keys, and IP addresses.

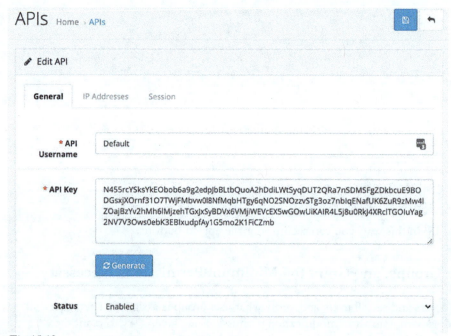

Fig: 15.10

Always use the latest Opencart version, theme, modules, and extensions

It is better to use the latest Opencart version, theme, modules, and extensions. You may have problems getting the upgraded version of your custom modules and extensions but if you don't update it then you risk the security.

Remove unused modules or extensions

Login to admin >> Extensions >> Installer >> You can see a list of modules that are installed. Remove unused modules or extensions. Similarly verify if old files and folders are remaining, especially for custom modules and themes.

Don't use nulled Opencart themes, modules, or extensions. Choose trustworthy plugins and theme providers, it can cost you some but it will protect you a lot.

Monitor your server logs

If you are using CPanel hosting then you can check the Resources Usage at **Login to Cpanel >> Metrics >> Resources Usage >> Snapshots.** You can check that resource limits are being reached, resulting in slow performance or errors. Often resource issues are due to scripting/plugins on your site, development work such as making changes, or an increased amount of traffic. You and your web developer can review the resource usage of your account and take steps to reduce the load. Some scripts that are running long by some IP address means there is some fishy going on, so make sure to keep on checking it and see if you can improve your code and scripts.

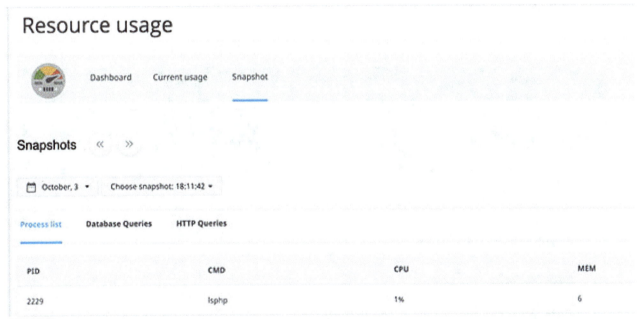

Fig: 15.11

Free Opencart website security check & malware scanner

You can check your website security and malware at https://sitecheck.sucuri.net/

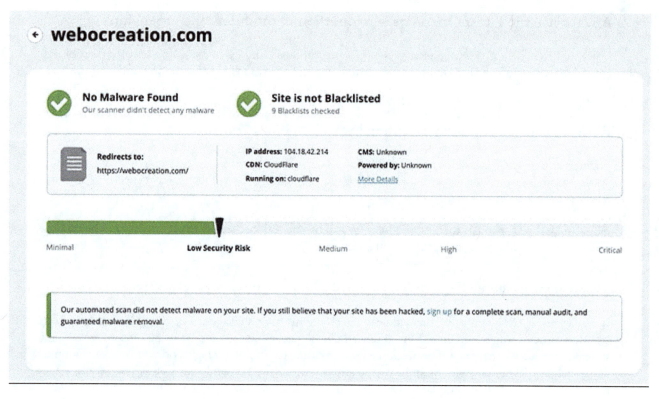

Fig: 15.12

Use HTTP security headers

You can get your HTTP security headers to report at https://securityheaders.com/

Fig: 15.13

Cross-Site Scripting (XSS)

If the programmer is tricky then in Opencart it is easy to add the JS script which may easily cause Cross-Site Scripting. Cross-site scripting (XSS) is when a malicious script is injected into a trusted website or application. The attacker uses this to send malicious code, typically browser-side scripts, to the end-user without them knowing it. The purpose is usually to grab cookies or session data or perhaps even rewrite HTML on a page. Go to admin>> Extensions >> Extensions >> Choose the Extensions Type as "Analytics" and see in the Google Analytics code field, if only required JS codes are added. If you see suspicious JS code then it is better to remove it.

Database Security and SQL Injections

Always use a strong database username and strong password. You can check this at config.php and admin/config.php, if you don't have then you need to change to a strong password and username.

Similarly, if you are using custom modules and there are database queries then you need to verify whether the queries are written properly, whether all the fields are escaped properly or not, and so on. One example of how they can inject the extra queries if you don't escape the fields is below:

YOUR_OTHER_QUERIES_customerid=0&directory=%2Febooks%2F1115.pdf&model=1115%27%2F% 2A%2A%2FAND%2F%2A%2A%2F**EXTRACTVALUE%282030%2CCONCAT%280x5c%2C0x4c634d 6c%2C%28SELECT%2F%2A%2A%2FMID%28%28IFNULL%28CAST%28email**%2F%2A%2A%2F AS%2F%2A%2A%2FNCHAR%29%2C0x20%29%29%2C1%2C22%29%2F%2A%2A%2FFROM%2F%2 A%2A%60.%%60%2F%2A%2A%%2F%2A%2A%2FBY%2F%2A%2A%2F%%60%2F%2A%2A%2FLIM IT%2F%2A%2A%2F8570%2C1%29%2C0x4c634d6c%29%29%2F%2A%2A%2FAND%2F%2A%2A%2F %276538%27%3D%276538&modelfinal=EREM+1115&order_id=30572&product_id=3389

See that bold section in the above queries, another query is concatenated and SQL injection is done.

Denial of Service

This is the most dangerous vulnerability, Denial of Service (DoS) exploits errors and bugs in the code to overwhelm the memory of website operating systems. Hackers have compromised millions of websites and raked in millions of dollars by exploiting outdated and buggy versions of Opencart software with DoS attacks. The hackers keep on running the code and your server CPU usage will be 100%, your server's Physical Memory Usage is full and the website will not be available for real users or customers.

One of the best recommendations is to use a reputable 3rd party security service like Cloudflare or Sucuri and be sure to use the code and scripts properly.

Backup

Be sure to make as much backup as possible.

Use Google Captcha or Basic Captcha

Using Google Captcha or basic captcha on the form also helps you remove spam and get emails that contain vulnerable links.

16. OPENCAT VQMOD TUTORIALS

In some earlier versions of Opencart 4, OCMOD was removed from the Opencart source code, planning to use only the event system for modifications but later OCMOD was added back. Although there is already OCMOD, some extension developers still use VqMod. We are showing you how to use VqMod with examples in Opencart, vqmod installation steps, configurations, and examples, and discuss what kind of issues can occur and their solutions. With this installation, you can use the vqmod XML file to override the core file without changing core files.

Download:

"vQmod™" (aka Virtual Quick Mod) is an override system designed to avoid having to change core files. The concept is quite simple... Instead of making changes to the core files directly, the changes are created as XML search/replace script files. These script files are parsed during page load as each "source" core file is loaded with the "include" or "require" php functions. Download VqMod for Opencart 4: https://github.com/vqmod/vqmod/releases

Installation steps of VqMod for Opencart 4

Following the steps below will install Vqmod for Opencart 4:

- Before doing anything please back up your Opencart installation so that you can revert if unexpected results happened.
- Download the VqMod from the https://github.com/vqmod/vqmod/releases
- Extract the zip that you download, vQmod-oc4-master.zip
- You will get the vqmod folder and readme file and copy the vqmod directory in your Opencart root directory, alongside the admin, catalog, extension, system, etc. directories.
- If you've renamed your admin directory, you'll have to do this bit manually for now:
  - Open vqmod/install/index.php and change $admin = 'admin'; on around line 33 to match your new admin directory name. We have used wpadmin, so that line is $admin='wpadmin'
  - Open vqmod/pathReplaces.php and change the line you'd add would be:
    // START REPLACES //
    $replaces[] = array('~^admin\b~', 'wpadmin');
    // END REPLACES //

Configuration:

Now, open your website and add /vqmod/install/ at the end of the URL something like https://demo.webocreation.com/vqmod/install/. If everything is correct, you will get messages like

VQMOD HAS BEEN INSTALLED ON YOUR SYSTEM!

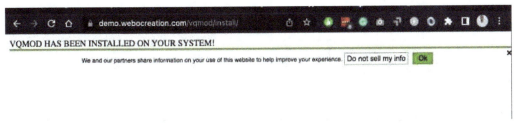

Fig. 16.1

Errors and Solutions:

1. Administrator index.php is not writeable

Administrator index.php not writeable

Fig 16.2

For this issue, first check and please make sure you replace your admin folder correctly on the vqmod/install/index.php and vqmod/pathReplaces.php, and then you can check the file permission if your server can write on the index.php file.

2. ERROR – COULD NOT DETERMINE Opencart PATH CORRECTLY

For this issue also, we need to make sure you replace your admin folder correctly on the vqmod/install/index.php and vqmod/pathReplaces.php

Example use of Vqmod in Opencart 4

Here is one demo XML file in which you show the "Special Offers" links in the main menu. Open the project in your text editor and go to vqmod folder and then the XML folder create a file named speciallink.xml and add the following lines of code:

```
<modification>
    <version>Opencart Version 4</version>
    <vqmver>4.0.0</vqmver>
    <author>Rupak Nepali</author>
    <code>SpecialLinkOnMenu</code>
    <file name="catalog/view/template/common/menu.twig" error="skip">
        <operation>
            <search position="after"><![CDATA[
```

```
        <ul class="nav navbar-nav">
    ]]></search>
    <add><![CDATA[
        <li class="nav-item"><a class="nav-link" href="index.php?route=product/special">Special
Offers</a></li>
        ]]></add>
    </operation>
  </file>
</modification>
```

Fig:16.3

Once, you add the above code and then refresh the frontend URL, then you will see a menu item added at the beginning of the Opencart top menu.

Special Offers

Fig: 16.4

In this way, you can use VqMod, know how to install vqmod, and its configurations, for example, and learn how to fix issues that may occur.

17. PRO TIPS FOR OPENCART DEVELOPERS

Activating twig debugging

Go to /system/library/template/twig.php and find this line: *$this->twig = new \Twig_Environment($loader, $config);* just above that find similar code and change the debug to true.

```
$config = [
    'charset'     => 'utf-8',
    'autoescape'  => false,
    'debug'       => true,
    'auto_reload' => true,
    'cache'       => DIR_CACHE . 'template/'
];
```

With this active now you can use the dump function in the twig files and see the output, to view all the variables and content you can use like below:

```
<pre>
    {{ dump() }}
</pre>
```

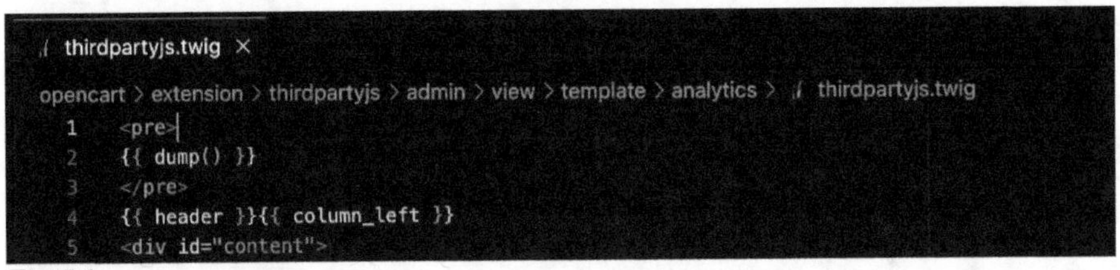

```
thirdpartyjs.twig ×

opencart > extension > thirdpartyjs > admin > view > template > analytics >  thirdpartyjs.twig
   1   <pre>
   2   {{ dump() }}
   3   </pre>
   4   {{ header }}{{ column_left }}
   5   <div id="content">
```

Fig 17.1

Master Product and Variant Product in Opencart

In Opencart we can create a variant product based on the master product. A product variant is a predefined option product. For example, let's say we add a product with red and blue options (product id 50), now we can create a variant based on this product and select the option red only to make the red variant product (product id 51 with master id 50).

How to add the product variant in Opencart?

Go to products listing or Catalog>>Products and click the dropdown near the edit button in the Action column and you will see the "Add Variant", click it and you are ready to add the variant.

Fig 17.2

Once you click the "Add Variant", all the data of the master product is copied and a new product is created where you can override the data as per your need. Please note that when you override the variant product data, the field data that is changed will not get replaced with the master product data when the master product data is changed and saved. If the field data is not overridden then when master product data is changed the changes will be seen on the variant product as well.

How to override the variant product data?

In the Variant product, you will see a toggle icon for every field where you can click On it and change the field data as per your need.

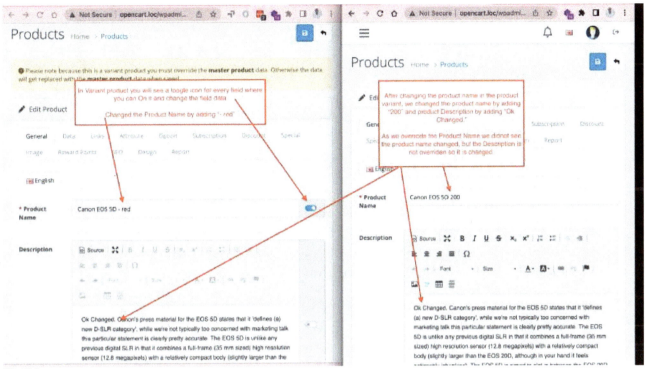

Fig 17.3

Let's say you change the product name but do not change the product description of the product variant, then when you change the product name and description of the master product the changes will be seen only on the product description but not on the product name. Variant products are pre-selected options so you cannot change the options on the variant product.

Note: if you save the product variant after the master product's data is changed then the variant product overridden data is replaced by the master product's data, so be careful.

Select the Option:

Fig 17.4

Change the SEO URL:

Add Product
General
Data
Links
Attribute
Option
Subscription
Discount
Special
Image
Reward Points
SEO
Design
Report
Do not use spaces, instead replace spaces with - and make sure the SEO URL is globally unique.
Stores
Keyword
Default
canon-eos-5d-red

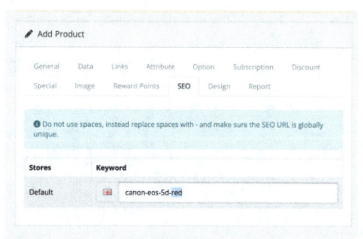

Fig 17.5

Now click save and you have added the product variant.

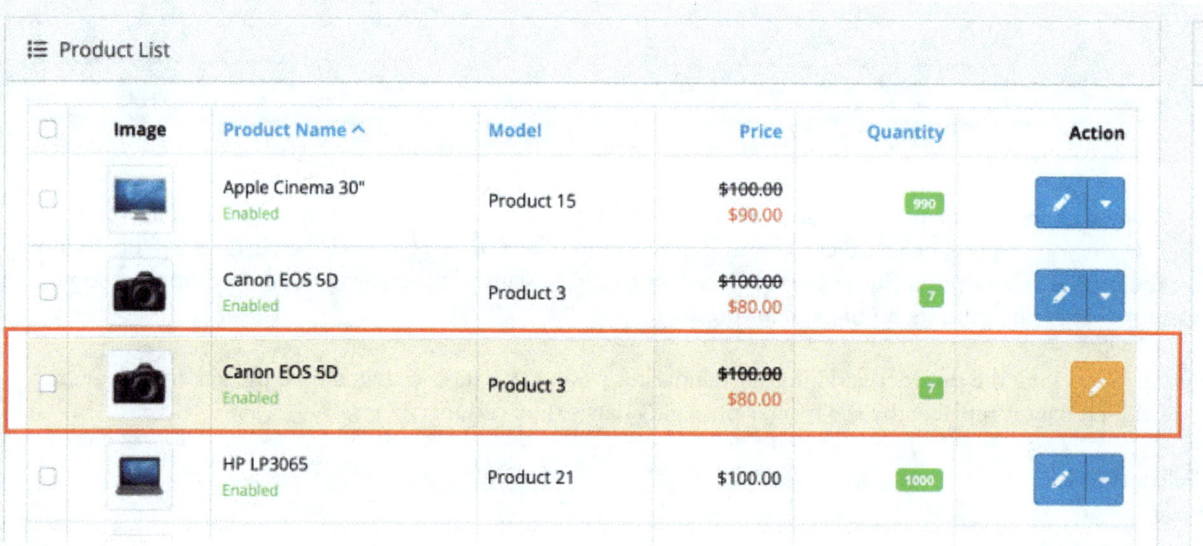

Product List
Image
Product Name
Model
Price
Quantity
Action
Apple Cinema 30"
Enabled
Product 15
$100.00
$90.00
990
Canon EOS 5D
Enabled
Product 3
$100.00
$80.00
7
Canon EOS 5D
Enabled
Product 3
$100.00
$80.00
7
HP LP3065
Enabled
Product 21
$100.00
1000

Fig 17.6

As the product variants are also added like new standalone products you can view them on the category page as well.

Customize layouts and positions to show different modules in Opencart

In this Opencart tutorial, we are showing how to customize layouts and positions to show different modules in Opencart. The layout is the process of setting out material on a page, in Opencart materials are modules. So if we want to show a set of modules in a specific URL or set of URLs then we can use Layouts and Positions.

Go to Admin >> Design >> Layouts where you can see all the layouts. By default, Opencart has the following layouts: Account, Affiliate, Category, Checkout, Compare, Contact, Default, Home, Information, Manufacturer, Product, Search and Sitemap

Inside each layout has four positions:

1. Column left
2. Content Top
3. Content Bottom
4. Column Right

Fig 17.7

You can add your custom layouts and show modules in that layout. Let's say you want to show the different layouts for each Category.

How to show different layouts for different pages in Opencart 4?

By default, there are 2–column layout sets for each category. We can add different layouts for different pages if it is set. We can assign different layouts for each category, product, and information page. Let's say you want to show two columns for the "**About us**" information page three columns for the "**Delivery Information**" information page and the default layout for the "**Privacy Policy**" information page.

Here are the steps:

- Go to Admin >> Design >> Layouts.
- Click "+: at the top right corner, to create the new layout. Say "Information 3 columns"
- Click Add route and enter catalog/information.
- To have 3 columns on the information page add some modules in Column Left and Column Right position, for example, Information and Category.
- Do the same for others

Now in the Admin >> Catalog >> Information >> Edit respective one (About us, Delivery Information or Privacy Policy) >> In the Design tab choose the required layout.

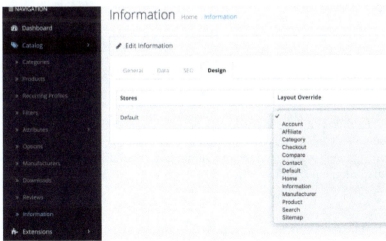

Fig 17.8

In this way, you can override the layout. What programmers/designers need to take care of positions and layout are:

1. Include CSS classes as per Opencart while creating the module so everyone can use your module, similarly while designing the theme be sure to use Opencart Bootstrap CSS so all custom modules that you use do not give design issues.

2. Be sure to add CSS that supports a three-column structure, two-column left column activated, two-column right column, and only one column activated.

   Before Bootstrap 5, you can see how Opencart used to handled main container class:

   {% if column_left and column_right %}
      {% set class = 'col-sm-6' %}
   {% elseif column_left or column_right %}
      {% set class = 'col-sm-9' %}
   {% else %}
      {% set class = 'col-sm-12' %}
   {% endif %}

   Now, after bootstrap 5, it is using the class="row" which we already defined in Chapter 6 title: **Using Bootstrap Grid System**

3. CSS adjustment for multi-column modules like:

   / fixed colum left + content + right*/*
   @media (min-width: 768px) {
      #column-left .product-layout .col-md-3 {
        width: 100%;
      }
      #column-left+#content .product-layout .col-md-3 {
        width: 50%;
      }
      #column-left+#content+#column-right .product-layout .col-md-3 {consider the layoutight .product-layout .col-md-3 {
        width: 100%;
      }
   }
   / fixed product layouts used in left and right columns */*
   #column-left .product-layout, #column-right .product-layout {
      width: 100%;
   }

In the above CSS you can see how bootstrap classes are overridden when the module is in the left column or the right column. So we also need to take care of them likewise while making modules.

As Opencart is using bootstrap, it is handling this with col-sm classes. As per the above code, it is assigning a different class. If both the column left and column right are activated which means three columns then the content middle will be col-sm-6, if only one column is activated either column left or column right then col-sm-9 is assigned. If none column is activated then col-sm-12 is assigned to the content middle and widths are adjusted accordingly.

Layouts in Opencart database tables:

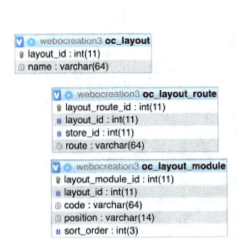
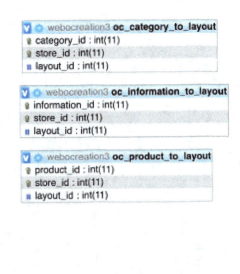

Fig 17.9

Taking layout-related database tables into consideration we can see that layout has the name. Each layout can have multiple routes as per the store. The layout can have many modules for each different position. Each page can use the layout as we see a layout id in the category, information, product, etc. So, if you are creating the pages then take the layout into consideration.

See all the variables that are available in the twig template

In Opencart, we can see all the variables that are available in the twig template by just adding the following code to the twig page.

```
<ol>
        {% for key, value in _context  %}
        <li>{{ key }}</li>
        {% endfor %}
</ol>
```

Or you can just simply activate the twig debug and us dump function {{ dump() }}

For e.g., if we want to see all the variables that are on the account login page, then open catalog/view/theme/default/template/account.twig and paste the above code now will be like below:

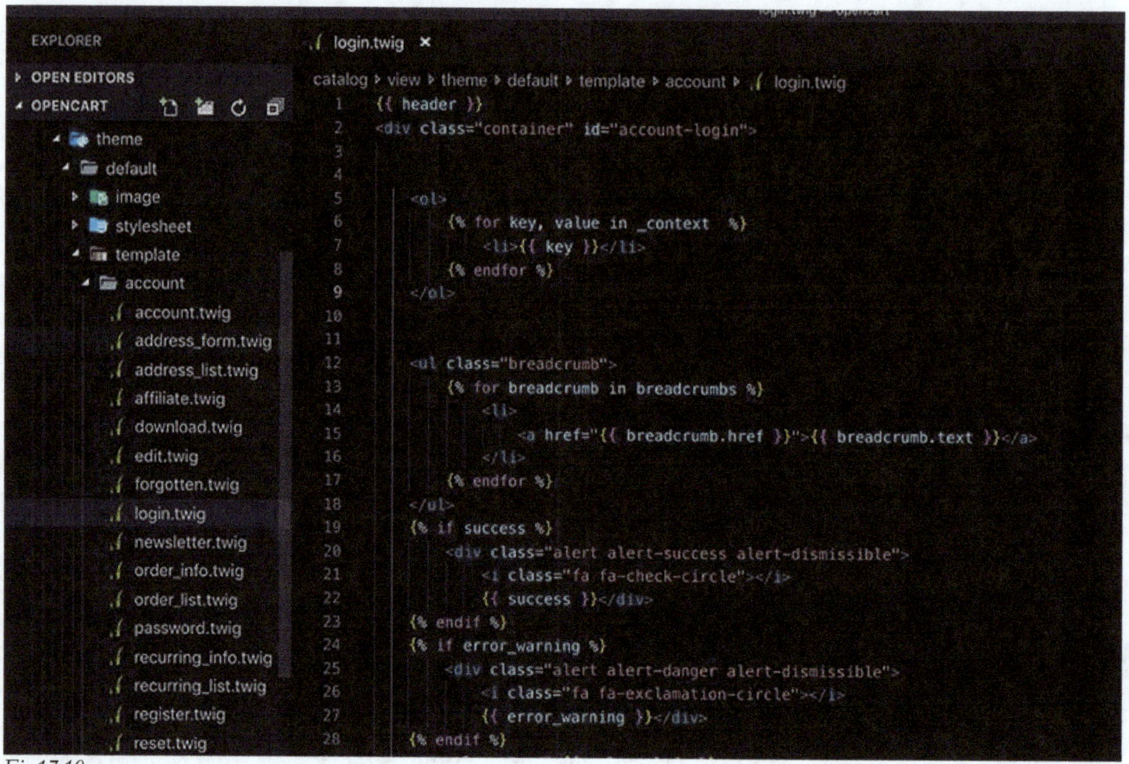

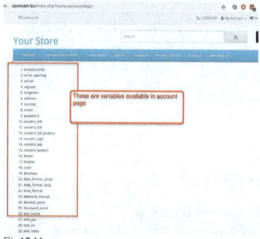

Fig 17.10

Now the output will be like the below:

Fig 17.11

How does Affiliate work in Opencart?

An affiliate program is a marketing strategy to increase sales by increasing the number of partners who will sell store products for commission. In Opencart 4 we will show how affiliate works. We added the customer as an affiliate, in Opencart 2 affiliate needs to be registered separately. The whole flow of the affiliate is shown in the following image:

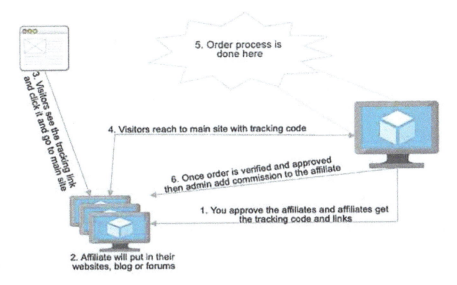

Fig 17.12

How is the affiliate registered in Opencart 4?

The Affiliate link is in the footer of the extra column in the default Opencart theme. The link to register is https://YOURURL/index.php?route=affiliate/login, then the visitors of the website can register for the Affiliate program which will become a customers as well. They will get an email with the tracking code.

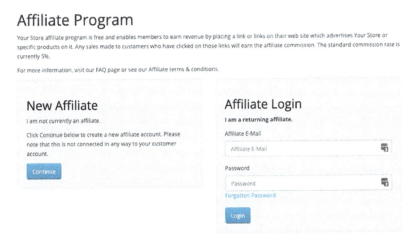

Fig 17.13

The customer can also register for the Affiliate from the Customer Dashboard.

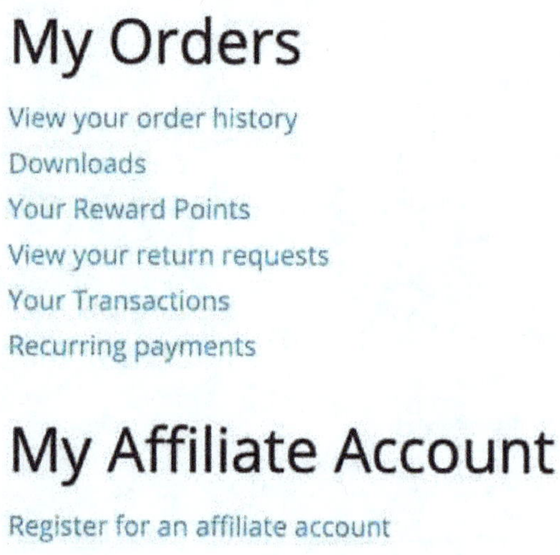

My Orders

View your order history

Downloads

Your Reward Points

View your return requests

Your Transactions

Recurring payments

My Affiliate Account

Register for an affiliate account

Fig 17.14

How to activate the affiliate for the already registered customers?

Go to Admin >> Customers >> Customers >> Edit the customer with whom you want to make an affiliate >> Click on the Affiliate tab enter the details and choose Status to enable:

Fig 17.15

Save it and the customer becomes an affiliate. Sometimes approval is needed if the setting "Affiliate Required Approval" is enabled at admin >> System >> Settings >> Edit your store >> In the Options tab there is an Affiliates section where there are multiple options to select for the affiliates as shown in the image below:

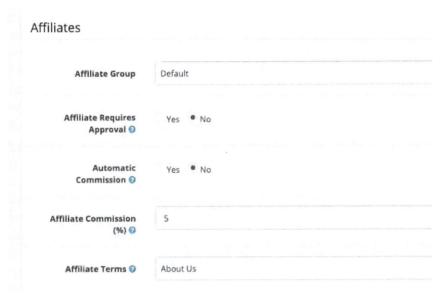

Fig 17.16

How does the affiliate use the URL on their websites blogs or forums?

Login to the front as a customer or affiliate then go to "**My Account**" and click "**Custom Affiliate Tracking Code**", you will see the tracking code, tracking link generator, and tracking link.

Don't change the tracking code as this is unique for you and if you change then the old URL will not work. Then in the tracking link generator enter the product name that you want to link, it will autocomplete your product, select it and the Tracking link is showing which is the link that you will use in the websites or blogs or forums.

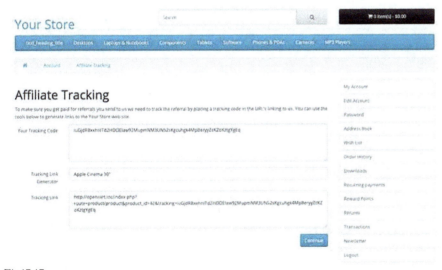

Fig 17.17

Your tracking link is
http://YOURURL/index.php?route=product/product&product_id=42&tracking=YOURTRACKING

CODE, if you want to redirect to the home page of the website then it will be like http://Opencart.loc/index.php?tracking=YOURTRACKINGCODE. The Opencart will set the cookie "tracking" with your tracking code for 1000 days. If you want to change those days then go to catalog >> controller >> startup >> startup.php and find the following code:

// Tracking Code
if (isset($this->request->get['tracking'])) {
    setcookie('tracking', $this->request->get['tracking'], time() + 3600 * 24 * 1000, '/');
    $this->db->query("UPDATE `" . DB_PREFIX . "marketing` SET clicks = (clicks + 1) WHERE code = '" . $this->db->escape($this->request->get['tracking']) . "'");
}

Now change the *setcookie('tracking', $this->request->get['tracking'], time() + 3600 * 24 * 1000, '/');* time to your preferred seconds. It should be in seconds like if you want to set cookie only for 60 days then it will be time() + 3600 * 24 * 60 and so on.

How is the commission added to the affiliate?

When someone clicks the affiliate tracking link and reaches the website the cookie is set, once the order is complete the Affiliate amount is shown in the Admin >> Sales >> Orders like in the image below:

Fig 17.18

Now the affiliate will see the commission amount at their dashboard >> My Orders >> Your Transactions and they will see the amount there:

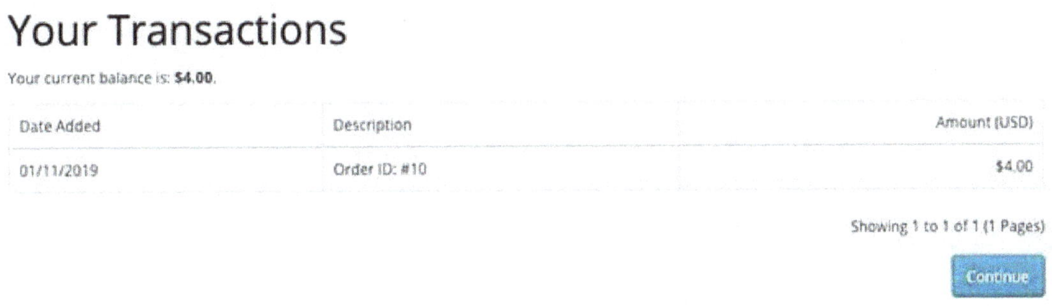

Your Transactions

Your current balance is: **$4.00**.

Date Added	Description	Amount (USD)
01/11/2019	Order ID: #10	$4.00

Showing 1 to 1 of 1 (1 Pages)

[Continue]

Fig 17.19

The current balance can be used as Store Credit to buy the products in the store. It will be like below:

Checkout

Step 1: Checkout Options

Step 2: Billing Details ▾

Step 3: Delivery Details ▾

Step 4: Delivery Method ▾

Step 5: Payment Method ▾

Step 6: Confirm Order ▾

Product Name	Model	Quantity	Unit Price	Total
HTC Touch HD	Product 1	1	$100.00	$100.00
			Sub-Total:	$100.00
			Flat Shipping Rate:	$5.00
			Store Credit:	$-4.00
			Total:	$101.00

[Confirm Order]

Fig 17.20

We didn't find a way to request a check or send it to Paypal although Opencart had the option, we hope this will be a manual process, for now, just contact the store owner once you have some balance.

What is the Order total in Opencart 4? How to apply and create them?

In Opencart Order total modules are those which decrease or increase the total price of the total order. Some of the order totals that decrease the total price are coupons, store credits, reward points, etc. Some of the order totals that increase the total price are Handling fees, low order fees, taxes, etc. You can see order totals by going to Admin >> Extensions >> Extensions >> Choose the extension type Order Totals, then you will see all the order totals. Some of the default order totals are the following:

- Coupon
- Store Credit
- Handling Fee
- Klarna Fee
- Low Order Fee
- Reward Points
- Shipping
- Sub-total
- Taxes
- Total
- Gift Voucher

How to install the Order total in Opencart?

Go to Admin >> Extensions >> Extensions >> Choose the extension type "Order Totals" and click the install button that you want to install and Edit it, Enable it and click Save.

Order totals affect the total price of the order so they are placed in the order total. You will find the order total at the shopping cart page and the confirmation page of the order.

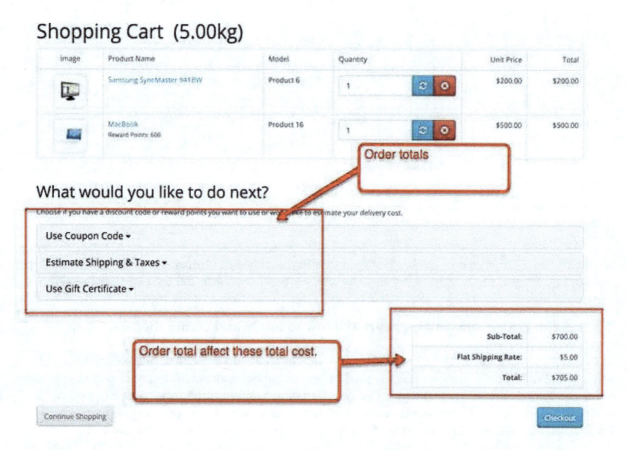

Fig 17.21

Why is shipping not showing in Opencart?

First, check if the shipping order total is enabled or not. If it is not enabled then we need to enable it. Next is to check for the Geozone setting of Opencart for the products.

How to apply and create the Order total in Opencart?

When we install the Order total modules then it is stored as 'total' code in the oc_extension database table. Check the following code to see how it pulls all the enabled Order total and applies it to the order total costs.

```
$results = $this->model_setting_extension->getExtensions('total');
foreach ($results as $key => $value) {
    $sort_order[$key] = $this->config->get('total_' . $value['code'] . '_sort_order');
}
array_multisort($sort_order, SORT_ASC, $results);
foreach ($results as $result) {
    if ($this->config->get('total_' . $result['code'] . '_status')) {
        $this->load->model('extension/total/' . $result['code']);
        // We have to put the totals in an array so that they pass by reference.
        $this->{'model_extension_total_' . $result['code']}->getTotal($total_data);
    }
}
```

We hope this post may help you understand the Order total of Opencart

How do reward points work in Opencart?

Go to the admin section >> Extensions >> Extensions >> Choose Order Total >> Then Install the Reward Points >> Edit and you can select Enabled or Disabled.

Reward Points Home › Extensions › Reward Points

✏ Edit Reward Points Total

Status	Enabled

Sort Order	2

Fig 17.22

How to set the reward points for each product?

Fig 17.23

In the image above, 5000 is the reward points that the customers can buy the product and 200 is the reward points that the customer gets on buying the product.

How this 200 reward point is added to the customer as in the example?

Go to Sales>>Order>>View the order that contains the reward gaining product and click "add the reward"

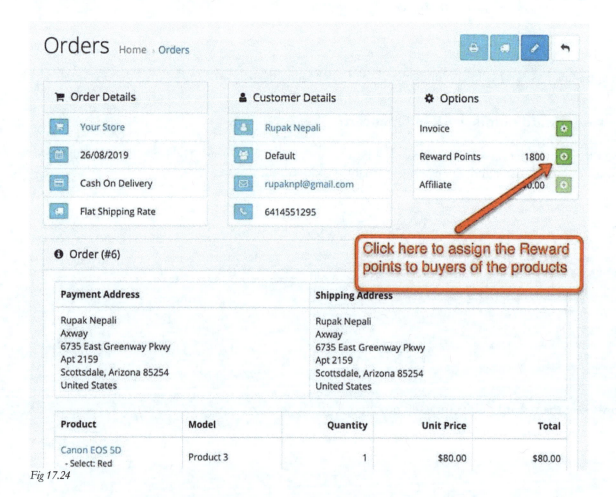

Fig 17.24

This means we have to process each order. If you don't see the Add the reward then it means there is a reward point for products in the respective order.

The administrator can directly provide reward points to the customer as well from the customer's sections. Go to Customers>> Customers >> Edit one >> Click the Reward Points tab and Insert the description and the Rewards points that the admin wants to assign to the customers.

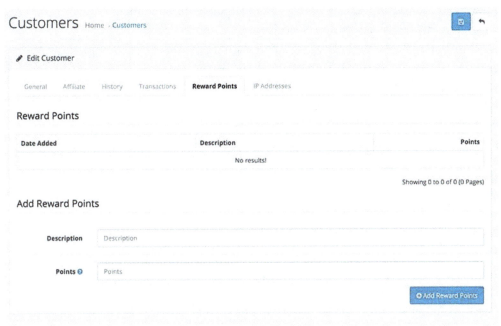

Fig 17.25

Customers can see their reward points by going to the Reward Points and they can view their details at:

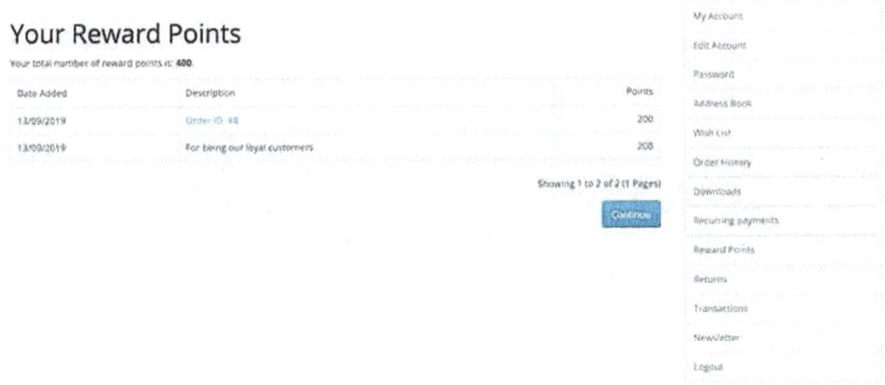

Fig 17.26

In this way, you can set up the Opencart reward points.

What is 'Zone Shipping' and how do we set it up?

Zone Shipping is simply shipping that is based on the different destinations, or geo zones, based on the weight of the total order. For example, if you're shipping from California USA. You can set a rate to other customers in other states, or other countries by setting up a zone for each destination and then setting the shipping price for each weight range from you to other places.

1. Set up a new zone in Admin->Configuration->Localisation->Geo Zones
2. Click on the "Insert" icon to add a new 'Geo Zone'
3. Call it "USA Shipping Zone" and click Save. You should now have a USA Shipping Zone on the list.
4. Click on the yellow folder icon to the left of the title
5. Click on the "Insert" icon to add a new 'Zone to Geo Zone'
6. From the 'Country' dropdown, choose 'United States'
7. From the 'Region / State' dropdown, choose an individual state, or choose 'All Zones' for the same rate to all 50 states & provinces
8. Click 'Save'.
9. Repeat this process for the UK, Australia, China, Japan, etc. anywhere you want to exclusively allow this type of shipping to.
10. Go to Extensions->Shipping, find 'Zone', and click the "wrench/spanner" icon to configure it
11. You should see text boxes for all your new zones. Enter the cost per weight range in each of the cost fields, based on the rates you want to use. The format is:
     Weight: Cost with multiple values separated by a comma: 5:2.00, 10:4.00

Using the above example (with lbs and $ for the example) would mean that
– Orders from 0-5.0lbs, the shipping cost is: $2.00
– Orders from 5.1-10.0lbs, the shipping cost is: $4.00
– Orders from 10.1lbs+ would not be eligible for zone shipping

How to customize the Opencart homepage?

In this Opencart guide, we are showing how to customize the Opencart 4 homepage and make changes to layouts, modules, and edit homepage content in Opencart 4. As the homepage of Opencart is made of modules, to change the home page layout in Opencart for demo data here are the steps: Go to admin >> Design >> Layouts >> Edit the Home Layouts >> You will see similar like below:

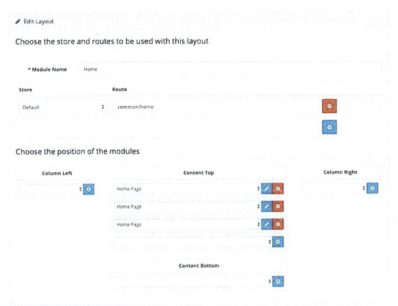

Fig 17.I 27

You can see which modules are active on the homepage, in the demo data of Opencart 4 there are three modules that are active only in the Content Top layout. These three modules in Opencart are the Slideshow module, the Featured Products module, and the Carousel module. You can add and remove the modules as per your requirement in the layouts.

Where can you find modules in Opencart 4?

Go to Admin >> Extensions >> Extensions >> Choose the Extension type "Modules", you will see all the modules here. Now see the Slideshow module and edit it. You will find the settings for the Slideshow in the image below:

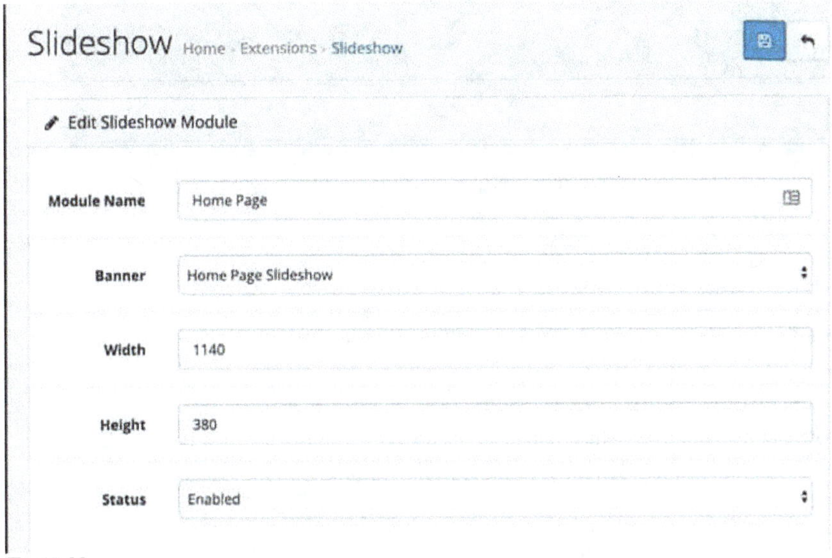

Slideshow Home · Extensions · Slideshow

✎ Edit Slideshow Module

Module Name	Home Page
Banner	Home Page Slideshow
Width	1140
Height	380
Status	Enabled

Fig 17.28

You can select the banner, give width and height, and change the status. Likewise, you can make changes in the Featured Products module and Carousel module. Similarly, you can activate the modules that you want to show on the home page and enable it. Then, add in the layouts.

Add conversion code on the success page of Opencart

Conversion codes are mostly added on the success page. Here are the steps to add conversions the Opencart way, it may long way but it is Opencart way taking layouts into consideration:

1. Go to admin >> Extensions >> Extensions >> Choose the extension type "Module" and install the Custom HTML module >> add new >> Enter module name >> Click the </> icon on description >> insert the JavaScript code >> Click the </> icon again >> select Enabled on status >> click Save.

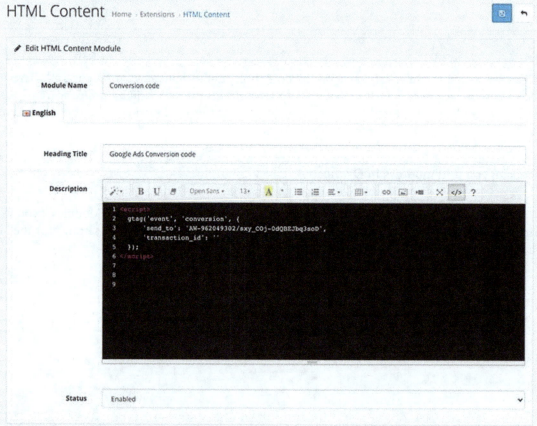

Fig 17.29

2. Now, go to admin >> Design >> Layouts >> Edit the checkout layout
3. Change the module name to "Checkout Cart"
4. In the route field change "checkout/%" to "checkout/cart"
5. Now, click add a new layout, then enter module name is "Checkout Checkout" and in the route field click "add new" button and add the route as "checkout/checkout" and then click Save.

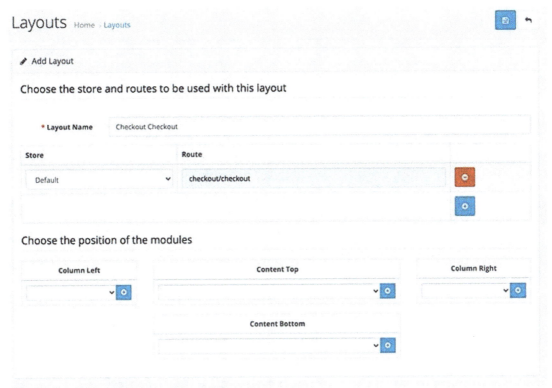

Fig 17.30

6. Similarly, click Add a new layout, then enter the module name as "Checkout Success" and in the route field click "add new" button, enter "checkout/success", then click the add button on the Content Bottom position and select the Conversion code HTML module, then click Save button.

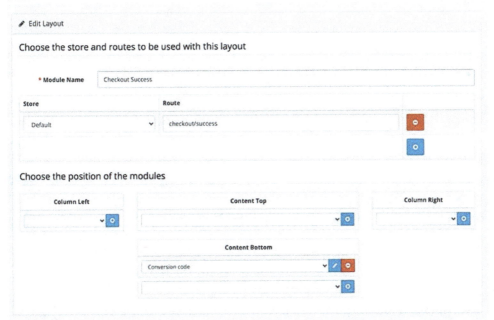

Fig 17.31

7. With the above steps, the conversion code is shown only on the success page.

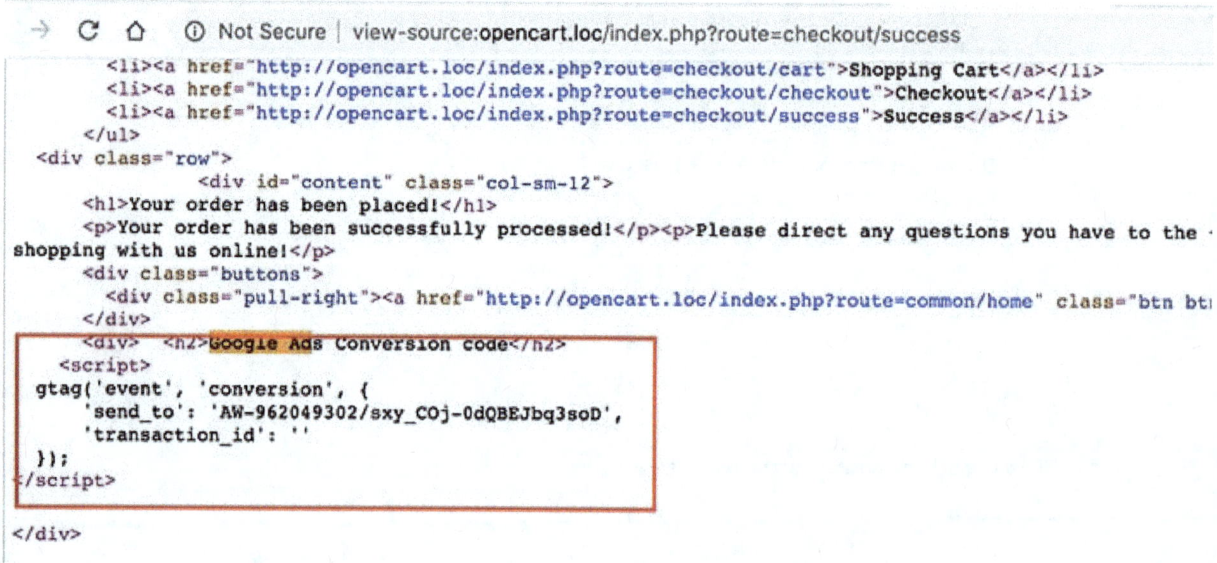

Fig 17.32

In this way, you can add conversion code on the success page only.

Currencies management in the Opencart 4 version with auto-update

Opencart 4 supports multi-currencies so with Opencart we can sell in any currency, anywhere in the world. Go to admin >> System >> Localization >> Currencies where you will see the currencies available for use in the storefront. In the store by default, there are Euro, Pound, and US dollars but only the US dollar is enabled by default.

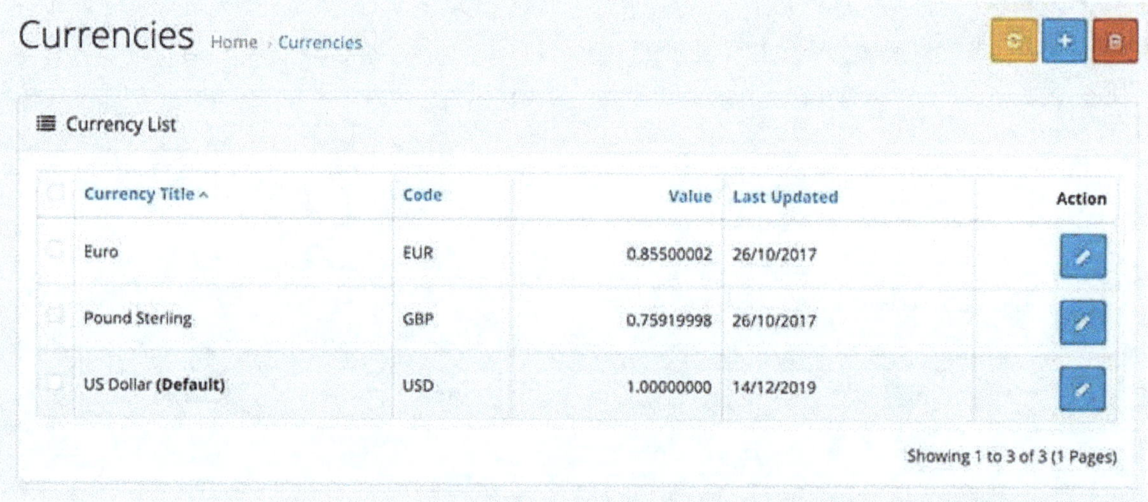

Fig 17.33

Default currencies in Opencart

The default currency is set to a value of 1. When you enter the product's price we need to enter it as per the default currency with value 1. Every value of the currency will be relative to this value as per the above image the value of the US Dollar is 1.0, and the Euro is calculated to be 0.85500002. The frontend price is calculated and converted as per the currency value which is 1. If Auto Update Currency is enabled then the currency is auto-updated.

DON'T CONFUSE WITH DEFAULT CURRENCY AND VALUE 1 OF CURRENCY

Here you need to enter the price worth with the currency value equal to 1. Don't enter the default currency value but need to enter the price of currency value equal to 1. Mostly they are the same but be sure the currency value is 1 and it is the default currency.

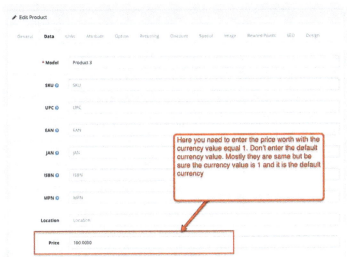

Fig 17.34

How to add the currency in Opencart 4?

To add the currency, go to admin >> System >> Settings >> Localization >> Currencies and click the Add New blue button and you will see the form below:

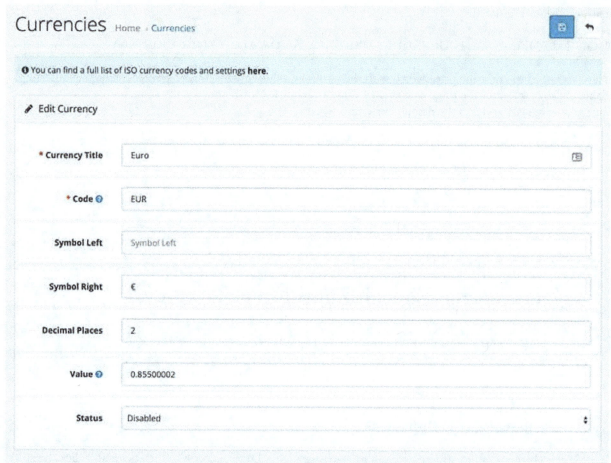

Fig 17.35

Default currency form Opencart

Currency Title: Enter the name of the currency that you want to show in the front end.
Code: The ISO currency code, you can get the currency code at
https://www.ibm.com/support/knowledgecenter/en/SSZLC2_7.0.0/com.ibm.commerce.payments.developer.doc/refs/rpylerl2mst97.htm
Symbol Left: You can find the currency symbol at https://www.xe.com/symbols.php and if you want to show the symbol to the left of the price of the product then add it here.
Symbol Right: You can find the currency symbol at https://www.xe.com/symbols.php and if you want to show the symbol to the right of the price of the product then add it here.
Decimal Places: The number of decimal places that you want to show in the front end.
Value: The default currency will be set to a value of 1 and other currency will be converted value.
Status: You can enable or disable the currency in the front end.

How to change the default currency in Opencart 4?

To change the default currency in Opencart 4, go to admin >> System >> Settings >> Edit the store >> then click the local tab and in the currency field change the currency that you want to make the default. Then, set your store to automatically update currencies. After that clear your browser cache to see the change and reset your existing cookies. Now your default currency in the Opencart 4 is set.

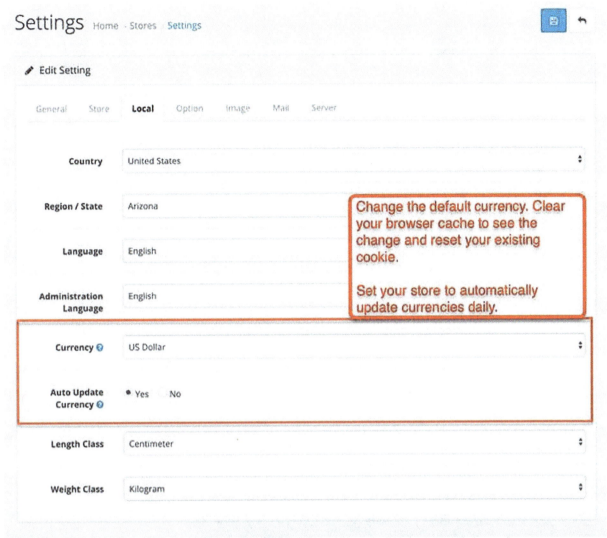

Fig 17.36

How do auto-update currencies exchange rate works in Opencart?

In Opencart 4, by default, there are auto-update currencies as per the currency rate converter engine "European Central Bank Currency Converter". To enable it, log in to admin >> System >> Settings >> Edit the store >> Local tab and enable Auto Update Currency field and select the Currency Rate Engine and Save. Now, your store is set to automatically update currencies daily.

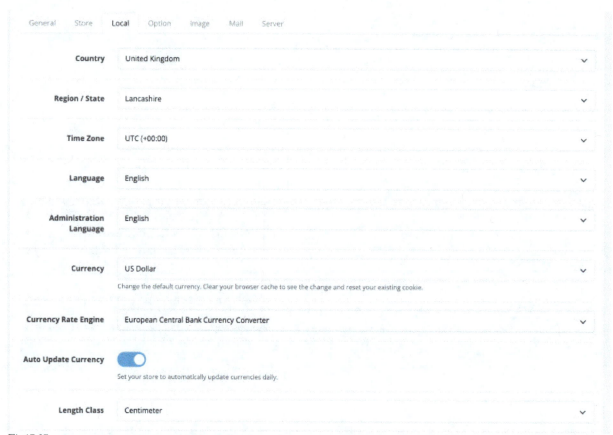

Fig 17.37

As we see Opencart is using this URL to get the currencies' value https://www.ecb.europa.eu/stats/eurofxref/eurofxref-daily.xml, as seeing the values it supports only some currencies so auto-update currencies may not be supported for all currencies.

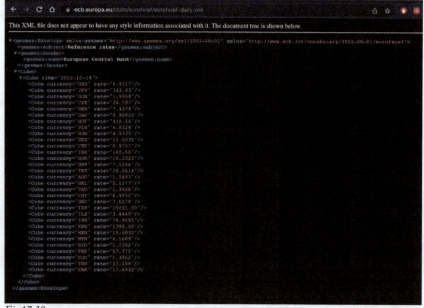

Fig 17.38

Fix the cron job so that it gets updated daily

If you are seeing the auto-update is not working then your cron job is not running, make sure it is running daily. To check the status of the cron jobs, log into admin >> Extensions >> Cron Jobs and see the date modified and you can run the cron jobs from there as well

Fig 17.39

Support Opencart code, Creating a pull request

You may want to support the Opencart open source and build your portfolio for that the following guidelines are useful for creating a pull request to support the OpenCart project. To streamline the review process and ensure efficiency, the Opencart team kindly requested that each pull request address only a single fix. This approach enables their code review team to evaluate and merge contributions more quickly and effectively. If you submit multiple commits in a single pull request and even a small part of the code is wrong they decline the whole pull request, because Git/Github does not allow them to cherry-pick which commits they accept inside a pull request. To create a pull request follow these simple steps. The examples will assume you are using TortoiseGit on Windows but most Git UI applications will follow similar steps.

This guide outlines the steps for contributing code changes to the OpenCart project through GitHub.

1. Fork the OpenCart Repository:

- Login to your GitHub account and navigate to the official OpenCart repository.
- Click the "Fork" button to create a personal copy in your GitHub account. This allows you to make changes and submit pull requests without affecting the main project.

2. Clone your Fork Locally:

- Use Git to clone your forked repository to your local development machine. This creates a working copy on your system.

3. Create and Switch to a Feature Branch:

- Within your local repository, utilize Git commands to create a new feature branch. Name the branch descriptively, such as patch-1.
- Ensure the branch is based on the upstream master branch and switch to the newly created branch for your development work.

4. Implement Changes and Test Thoroughly:

- Make the necessary code modifications to your chosen files.
- Always rigorously test your changes on a dedicated test environment (local or remote) to verify functionality and potential regressions.

5. Commit Changes with Descriptive Messages:

- Use Git to commit your changes locally.
- Craft detailed and informative commit messages that clearly describe the changes made.
- Include references to relevant external documentation and consider adding links to screenshots for improved clarity.

6. Push Changes and Create a Pull Request:

- Push your committed changes to your forked repository on GitHub.
- Locate the "Pull requests" link and initiate a new pull request.
- This will initiate a comparison between your feature branch (patch-1) and the upstream master branch.
- Review the changes and confirm the intended merge into the OpenCart master branch.
- Submit the pull request for review by the OpenCart development team.

7. Avoid Modifying Feature Branch:

- To maintain a clean development workflow, it's recommended to refrain from further commits to the feature branch after creating the pull request.
- This ensures a focused and streamlined review process.

8. Switching Branches and Creating New Features:

- If you need to implement additional changes, separate them from the existing feature branch.
- Use Git commands to switch back to the master branch in your local repository.
- Repeat steps 3-7 using a unique branch name (e.g., patch-2) for your new set of modifications.
- By following these guidelines, you can effectively contribute your code improvements to the OpenCart project while maintaining a clear and organized development workflow.

This guide outlines the steps for contributing code changes to the OpenCart project through GitHub. This way you can support the Opencart Open Source project.

18. COMMON ERRORS AND THEIR SOLUTIONS

This Opencart tutorial collects the most common errors that we face while developing and provides solutions for errors, try them and hope you can solve the issues

Cannot delete the admin folder in Opencart 4

This solution looks working, for now, change the following lines of code at admin/controller/common/security.php

foreach (glob(trim($next, '/') . '/{*,.[!.]*,..?*}', GLOB_BRACE) as $file) {

to following

foreach (glob($next . '/{*,.[!.]*,..?*}', GLOB_MARK|GLOB_BRACE) as $file) {

Blank white pages or 500 internal server error

Blank white pages are a PHP error that for some reason the error messages don't show because your server is not set up to display the errors.

1. Go to the admin>> System >> Setting >> Edit store >> Sand at the end where you see the Error handling choose Yes to "Display Errors ".
2. If you still don't see the error, open php.ini and add code below: *display_errors = 1; error_reporting = E_ALL; log_errors = 1;*
3. If you still don't see the error then open index.php and add the code below at the top (line 2): *ini_set('display_errors', 1); ini_set('log_errors', 1); error_reporting(E_ALL);*
4. Still see the error then, set your "Output Compression Level" to 0 in the System > Settings > Server tab.
5. If you still see the error, solve the issues but if you did not see the error then most probably it will be a Server error.
6. You can see error logs in the file also if you have enabled it.

Fig 18.1

Above most, it gets solved and the 500 Internal Server Error can be solved with a similar approach.

Undefined index/variable

An **undefined variable** in the source code of a computer program is a **variable** that is accessed in the code but has not been previously declared by that code. So for that, using "isset()" to check if the variable has been set will solve the issue.

Error Variant:
Notice: Undefined index: filter in **catalog/controller/product/category.php** online

Solution:
```
//$filter = $this->request->get['filter'];
if (isset($this->request->get['filter'])) {
        $filcan $this->request->get['filter'];
} else { $filter = '';}
```

Commenting *$filter = $this->request->get['filter'], and* checking with isset is one way to solve it.
If you get the issue while installing the modules or extensions then you need to check the code or solve the issues or contacting the developer can also be another solution.

Undefined function/method

Undefined function/method errors are seen when you call those functions or methods that are not defined and not found. IE_ERROR: A fatal error that causes script termination "Fatal error: Call to undefined function" or "Fatal error: Call to undefined method". It happens if files are not found or the extensions are not compatible with your Opencart version. Solutions can be below:

Error Variant:
Related to Opencart core files

- ○ **Fatal error**: Uncaught Error: Call to undefined method DB\MySQLi::query()
- ○ **Fatal error**: Uncaught Error: Call to undefined method Cart\Cart::getProducts()
- ○ **Fatal error**: Uncaught Error: Call to undefined method ControllerAccountLogin::validate() in …/catalog/controller/account/login.php:54

Go to the file and check whether the function or methods are defined there.

Headers already sent

Error Variant: Warning: **Cannot modify header information – headers already sent** by (output started at

188

/public_html/config.php:31) in /path/public_html/index.php online.

Solution: Remove spaces at the beginning and end of the file mentioned. Like in the above error check with the config.php

Session Issue: Some of the problems include:

1. The product on the cart is self-cleared.
2. The product on the cart is cleared after the user logs in.
3. No items stored at the product compare.
4. Opencart admin always asks to log in and gets the message "Invalid token session. Please log in again".

Error variant: Warning: **session_start ()** [function.session-start]: open (/tmp/…, O_RDWR) **failed: No such file or directory (2)** in /path/public_html/system /library /session.php on line

Solution:

1. Open php.ini and add code below: session.save_path = /tmp;
2. If the solution above does not work, contact your host and ask them how to set session.save_path.

Allowed Memory Size Exhausted

This error happens because your memory is not enough to execute the PHP code (uploading large images, deleting a lot of products, sending mass emails, etc). Increasing the memory allocated for PHP will solve the issue.

Error variant: Fatal error: the **Allowed memory size** of 1111 bytes **exhausted** (tried to allocate 1111 bytes) in /path/public_html/system/library/image.php on line

Solution:

1. Edit php.ini and set memory_limit = 128M;
2. Or put code below to .htaccess php_value memory_limit 128M
3. If the above does not work then contacting the hosting providers is only the solution where they can increase the number.

- **Warning: Use of undefined constant DIR_STORAGE – assumed 'DIR_STORAGE' (this will throw an Error in a future version of PHP) in …/config.php on line**

Some other errors that you can face are below

Error: Calls to magic methods are not allowed!

```
// Stop any magical methods being called
if (substr($this->method, 0, 2) == '__') {
    return new \Exception('Error: Calls to magic methods are not allowed!');
}
```

Error: Could not call product/category

```
// Initialize the class
if (is_file($file)) {
    include_once($file);
    $controller = new $class($registry);
} else {
    return new \Exception('Error: Could not call ' . $this->route . '/' . $this->method . '!');
}
```

Error: Could not load model

```
if (!$this->registry->has('model_' . str_replace('/', '_', $route))) {
    $file = DIR_APPLICATION . 'model/' . $route . '.php';
    $class = 'Model' . preg_replace('/[^a-zA-Z0-9]/', '', $route);
    if (is_file($file)) {
        include_once($file);
        $proxy = new Proxy();
        // Overriding models is a little harder so we have to use
        //  PHP's magic methods
        // In future version we can use runkit
        foreach (get_class_methods($class) as $method) {
            $proxy->{$method} = $this->callback($this->registry, $route . '/' . $method);
        }
        $this->registry->set('model_' . str_replace('/', '_', (string)$route), $proxy);
    } else {
        throw new \Exception('Error: Could not load model ' . $route . '!');
    }
}
```

Error: Could not load library or Error: Could not load helper

Error: Could not load cache adaptor Memcache/Redis/APC cache!

```
$class = 'Cache\\' . $adaptor;
if (class_exists($class)) {
    $this->adaptor = new $class($expire);
} else {
    throw new \Exception('Error: Could not load cache adaptor ' . $adaptor . ' cache!');
}
```

Error: Could not load database adaptor mpdo/mssql/mysql/mysqli/postgre!

```
$class = 'DB\\' . $adaptor;
if (class_exists($class)) {
    $this->adaptor = new $class($hostname, $username, $password, $database, $port);
} else {
    throw new \Exception('Error: Could not load database adaptor ' . $adaptor . '!');
}
```

Error: Could not make a database connection using this username and password

Error: Could not connect to database Opencart

Error: PHP GD is not installed!

```
if (!extension_loaded('gd')) {
    exit('Error: PHP GD is not installed!');
}
```

Error: Could not load image filename! Error: Invalid session ID!

Warning: The install folder still exists and should be deleted for security reasons!

- Installed bad extension, pressed refresh in the modification, and both admin panel and site are down

Remove it from the database, then open config.php and find what is the value defined for storage. Go to that storage/ folder, then go to modify and remove folders, similarly go to upload/ folder and see if there are folders if you have, remove it also. With this, it will remove the cached files and folder. Then, you can access your admin again.

Fatal error uncaught exception

Fatal error: Uncaught Exception: Error: Table '....oc_session' doesn't exist in engine
Error No: 1932
SELECT `data` FROM `oc_session` WHERE session_id = '....' AND expire > 1548638620 in .../system/library/db/mysqli.php:40 Stack trace: #0 .../system/library/db.php(45): DB\MySQLi->query('SELECT `data` F...') #1

For these errors to solve creating a database table will solve most of the issues

Fatal error: Uncaught Exception: Error: Could not load database adaptor DB_DRIVER!

Email is not working in Opencart – ways to solve

As we see some Opencart users are complaining that their email is not working in Opencart and are not able to see the Contact Us form message or the order message or other updates. We have listed some of the ways to fix them.

Email code in Opencart

Whenever the Mail class is instantiated like below and called the send method then you can say Opencart is sending an email. Example email code is:

```
mail = new Mail($this->config->get('config_mail_engine'));
$mail->parameter = $this->config->get('config_mail_parameter');
$mail->smtp_hostname = $this->config->get('config_mail_smtp_hostname');
$mail->smtp_username = $this->config->get('config_mail_smtp_username');
$mail->smtp_password = html_entity_decode($this->config->get('config_mail_smtp_password'), ENT_QUOTES, 'UTF-8');
$mail->smtp_port = $this->config->get('config_mail_smtp_port');
$mail->smtp_timeout = $this->config->get('config_mail_smtp_timeout');
$mail->setTo($customer_info['email']);
$mail->setFrom($this->config->get('config_email'));
$mail->setSender($store_name);
$mail->setSubject($subject);
```

$mail->setText($this->load->view('mail/customer_approve', $data));
$mail->send();

You can find these codes in admin/controller/mail/forgotten.php, catalog/controller/mail/register.php, catalog/controller/mail/order.php, catalog/controller/mail/affiliate.php, etc.

Check the email settings again

Login to admin of Opencart >> System >> Settings >> Edit the store that the email is not sending >> Click the Store tab >> Check if the email is set or not.

Fig 18.2

This email is the reply-to email.

Now, click the Mail tab, here are the settings to enter the email details.

Mail Engine: You can choose either Mail or SMTP in the Mail engine. Only choose 'Mail' unless your host has disabled the PHP mail function.

Mail: When you choose the Mail option, enter your email in the Mail Parameters. It is always best to enter the email of your website rather than using Gmail email or other email clients. If you send emails from other emails than your website then receivers can take it as spam. Like in the example: we use info@webocreation.com. If you choose Mail then you don't need to enter the SMTP details.

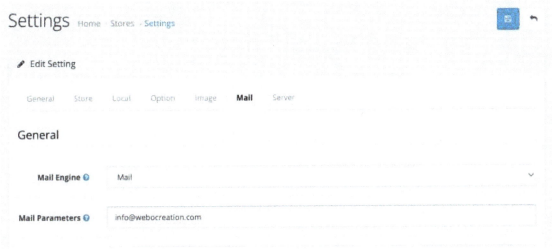

Fig 18.3

Sometimes, you need to enter the Mail Parameters as *-f info@webocreation.com*

SMTP:

You can use third-party email services that provide SMTP to send an email. All SMTP provides the following information

1. SMTP Hostname
2. SMTP Username
3. SMTP Password
4. SMTP Port

Here is one example, one of the SMTP providers provides the following information:

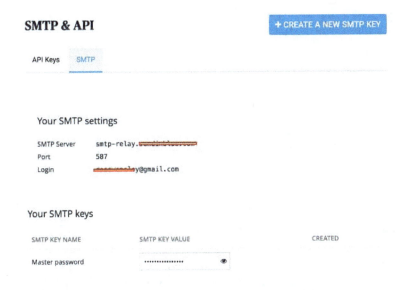

Fig 18.4

Enter the above SMTP settings in the Opencart by choosing the Mail engine as SMTP

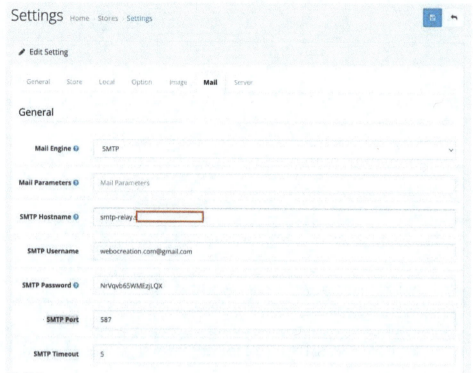

Fig 18.5

Every SMTP provider gives you the above information. The only thing is it can cost you extra.

Check Mail Alerts settings: Go to admin >> System >> Settings >> Edit store >> Mail tab >> Mail Alerts section

Fig 18.6

If you did not check the checkboxes for the one that you want to be alerted then these need to be checked.

Check all Events are set properly for Opencart 4: In Opencart 4 all mail needs to be set as Events in Opencart. Go to admin >> Extensions >> Events and check if all of the below events are added or not.

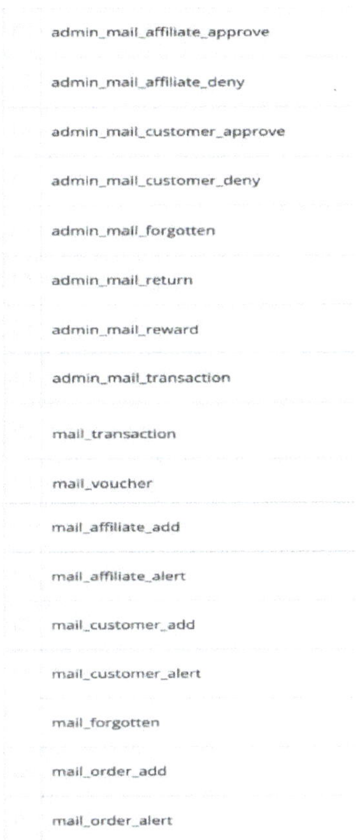

admin_mail_affiliate_approve

admin_mail_affiliate_deny

admin_mail_customer_approve

admin_mail_customer_deny

admin_mail_forgotten

admin_mail_return

admin_mail_reward

admin_mail_transaction

mail_transaction

mail_voucher

mail_affiliate_add

mail_affiliate_alert

mail_customer_add

mail_customer_alert

mail_forgotten

mail_order_add

mail_order_alert

Fig 18.7

With the above setting, an email should be sent if all servers' settings are good.

Server checking for email issues

Check for MX records:

Check if MX records are added for your domain or not. You can look for an online tool that checks for MX records. Here is one example:

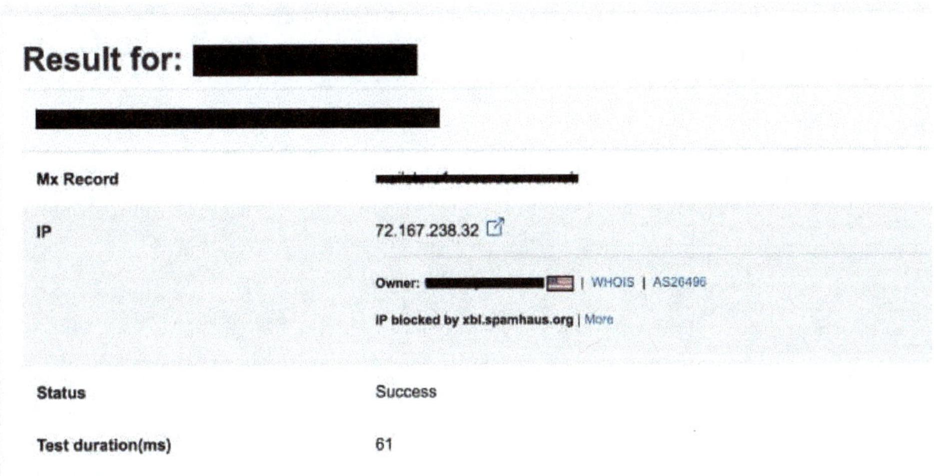

Result for: ▬▬▬▬▬▬

▬▬▬▬▬▬▬▬▬▬

Mx Record	▬▬▬▬▬▬▬▬▬▬▬▬
IP	72.167.238.32
	Owner: ▬▬▬▬▬▬	WHOIS	AS26496
	IP blocked by xbl.spamhaus.org	More
Status	Success
Test duration(ms)	61

Fig 18.8

If you did not have the MX records then you need to add them.

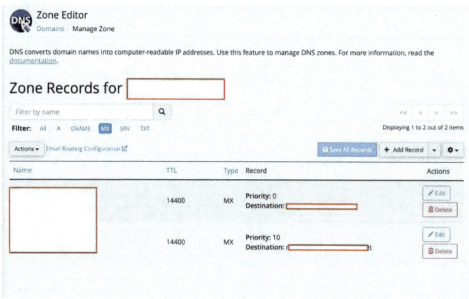

Fig 18.9

Once your MX records are added, now is the time to check for Email Routing

If cPanel:

If you are sending email from your server and you have chosen Mail as "Mail Engine" then check for Email Routing in the server and see whether the Email routing is configured to Local Mail Exchanger. But if you are using SMTP then the Email routing needs to be configured to Remote Mail Exchanger.

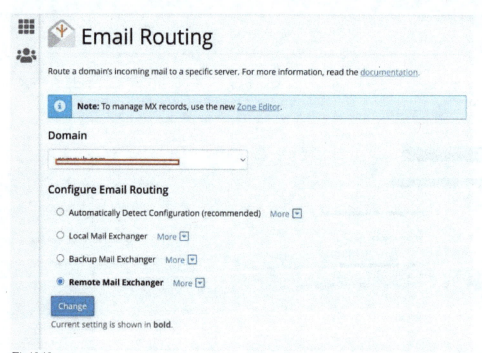

Fig 18.10

Check the email quota of your server

Most email servers have some email quota so if you reach that number they block sending the email, so verifying with the hosting provider is a way to check as well. Sometimes you get an email like the one below from your hosting provider.

*This message was created automatically by mail delivery software. A message that you sent could not be delivered to one or more of its recipients. This is a permanent error. The following address(es) failed: Domain ****.com has an outgoing mail suspension. Message discarded.*

Check if your hosting provider blocked the email services

Sometimes hosting providers or servers block the email services and they even block the third-party services or SMTP, they need to unblock the mail services, so ask them to unblock it. See one example they have posted on their website:

Upon checking the logs, we see that the email services were suspended for sending more than 1000 messages in the past 24 hours on November 19th, 2020 which was 2 years ago. We do have an email sending limit on our shared/reseller hosting which is 500 emails per hour, and 1000 emails per day for an account in which exceeding the limit causes email services to suspend.

Check your mail filter settings

If you don't receive mail from a particular email you can whitelist it in your mail filter and check the spam folder as well.

If you guys find any errors then you can email us at webocreation.com@gmail.com with all the steps to reproduce and we will help you as we find the solution.

USEFUL LINKS

Join us at https://webocreation.com to download the complete code example and you can also ask questions and comment about this book or other Opencart and eCommerce blog posts. You can submit or report issues, and errata and seek additional advice. You can also directly email us at webocreation.com@gmail.com

https://www.opencart.com/

https://github.com/opencart

https://docs.opencart.com/en-gb/introduction/

https://www.docker.com/get-started

https://github.com/opencart/opencart/wiki/Creating-a-pull-request

https://github.com/opencart/opencart/blob/master/docs/database/OpenCart%20-%20DB%20Schema.mwb

https://github.com/opencart/opencart/blob/master/docs/database/OpenCart%20-%20DB%20Schema.pdf

https://webocreation.com/how-to-build-a-free-ecommerce-website-using-opencart-4-user-manual-in-2024/

https://webocreation.com/opencart-tutorial/

https://github.com/opencart/opencart/wiki

https://sitecheck.sucuri.net/

https://securityheaders.com/

https://www.cloudflare.com/

https://www.ibm.com/docs/en

https://www.w3schools.com/tags/ref_language_codes.asp

https://developer.chrome.com/docs/extensions/reference/api/i18n#concepts_and_usage

https://www.w3schools.com/tags/ref_language_codes.asp

https://getbootstrap.com/docs/5.3/getting-started/introduction/

https://webocreation.com/ocmod-documentation

https://git-scm.com/

https://demo.webocreation.com/

https://rupaknepali.com.np/

https://www.brokenlinkcheck.com/

https://business.google.com/locations

https://www.php.net/supported-versions.php

https://github.com/vqmod/vqmod/releases